FLORENCE
The city and its art
by Luciano Berti
Sovrintendente per i Beni Artistici e Storici di Firenze
Preface by Sir Harold Acton

Scala Books
Distributed by Harper & Row, Publishers

Merry Christmas
to Cathy from [symbols]
December 25, 1981

Preface

It is an honour to introduce so succinct and scholarly an outline history of Florence as Dr. Luciano Berti's. Every visitor may respond to the visual magic of the city in a different manner, but Dr. Berti provides him with the salient facts of its development and fruition which will enhance his appreciation of the *genius loci*.

When we consider the vicissitudes of its past remote and recent, the decapitation of its 150 private towers in the thirteenth century and the too frequent ravages of party faction, it seems miraculous that so much beauty has survived. Some maintain that the flood of 1966 wrought more havoc than the last world war, but the destruction of all its bridges save the Ponte Vecchio, and of the medieval area surrounding it, was as tragic as it was avoidable. Fortunately Florentine good taste defeated those Philistines who wanted to replace the beautiful Ponte Santa Trinita with a modern substitute. The scrupulous rebuilding of Ammannati's masterpiece with as much of the original material as could be salvaged was a triumph for which we should all be grateful. The flood of 1966 caused greater damage to paintings, sculpture, libraries and furniture, but thanks to Florentine pluck and pertinacity and the active sympathy of foreign collaborators, far more was saved than could have been foreseen. New techniques of restoration and conservation were introduced, and they are still being perfected. Here indeed one is persuaded to believe in the survival of the fittest.

A quotation from Samuel Rogers's long-forgotten poem *Italy*, (of which nearly four thousand copies were sold within a year of its publication in 1830), has pride of place in Augustus Hare's equally forgotten guide to Florence, and it expresses neatly what many still feel in 1979:

"Of all the fairest Cities of the Earth
None is so fair as Florence. 'Tis a gem
Of purest ray; and what a light broke forth,
When it emerged from darkness! Search within,
Without; all is enchantment! 'Tis the Past
Contending with the Present; and in turn
Each has the mastery."

Yes, it is the past contending and blending with the present that exerts so potent a fascination on sensitive visitors to Florence, though their reasons for coming might be strangely mixed. When surfeited with the past, whose historical associations confront them not only in buildings which have defied the centuries but also in public squares and narrow streets, apart from the churches and museums, they could always turn to the bustling, vociferous present. Gucci, Pucci and Ferragamo contend with the Uffizi and Pitti galleries. Spiritually as well as materially the past impinges on the present. How often we notice that the passengers on streets and buses, both old and young, resemble their fifteenth-century forebears in Ghirlandaio's frescoes, and on closer acquaintance their general outlook is similar. They tend to dislike uniformity and mass production. They remain individuals, keenly critical, cautious, frugal, impatient of hypocrisy and facile sentiment. Because of their meticulousness Carducci described the Florentines as the Chinese of Italy, and I was forcibly struck by the comparison when I returned here after seven years in Peking. Bernard Berenson with his genial twinkle used to say of Arthur H. Smith's *Village Life in China* (1899): "it is an excellent study of village life in Tuscany."

The paradox applies especially to the Florentine artisan, proud of his native skill and ancient traditions. Which does not signify that he lacks originality and fresh ideas. In the fifteenth century which, as Dr. Berti justly observes, "determined the unique features of Florence . . . the serene refinement of plastic forms and lineal sobriety whose influence spread through Italy and thence to the rest of Europe," that eminently "universal man" Leon Battista Alberti chose the winged eye for his emblem: an open eye surmounted by two wings. How typically Florentine! From the profuse works of art to Galileo's instruments in the Science Museum, including his telescopes, clocks and astrolabes, the winged eye follows us with mesmeric intensity.

After Waterloo a swarm of frustrated English travellers came to Florence, and many stayed on to write about it or merely to economize in comfort. As the nineteenth century advanced the English colony became the largest in the peninsula. American as well as English painters, sculptors, scholars and antiquarians arrived in greater number since Ruskin had roused them with his resonant trumpet. Perhaps the most interesting of American expatriates was James Jackson Jarves who arrived in 1852 and, observing that Florence, the capital of the Grand Duchy of Tuscany, was "seductive to even a Republican imagination," stayed there at longer intervals until his death in 1887. His friends despised his pioneering collection of Tuscan Primitives which may now be enjoyed at Yale University.

"I never pass Giotto's Campanile without feeling my heart lightened, as if a celestial ray had descended upon me," he wrote after fifteen years of residence. "It might have been let down from heaven itself... When sorrowing or suffering I go to the Duomo, walk about it, and am comforted in its presence, not from any association of creed, but because it is a triumphant expression of the great human soul in its belief in the Infinite."

Until Ruskin flashed his torch on the special virtues of Giotto and his followers such seventeenth-century painters as Carlo Dolci and Guido Reni were regarded as supreme by the sentimental sightseer. Giotto had then to be rediscovered; so had Fra Angelico and Botticelli; which is hard for us to realize today. Unfortunately Ruskin's moralistic attitude driven to excess, renders him unpalatable to the amoral twentieth century. In spite of his Victorian rhetoric and dogmatic preaching he was intuitively right about the earliest Tuscan painters and sculptors, and it is regrettable that his vision became clouded when he examined the Renaissance, so that he dismissed Ghirlandaio's frescoes in Santa Maria Novella as "goldsmith's rubbish." The importance of his message in a materialistic age (though it seems less materialistic than ours, with our slavish worship of things, of products, as Solzhenitsyn remarked), was that art is not a superfluous luxury which we can afford to dispense with. Without art we are wretched starvelings or robots. The Greeks of Periclean Athens understood this, and after the centuries of darkness following the break-up of the Roman Empire it was in Florence that Greek humanism was reborn.

For a broader and more concrete interpretation of Florentine art than Ruskin's we must turn to the writings of Bernard Berenson. Applying a severe discipline to his studies which required, as he wrote, "the first-hand observation of the naturalist, the analysis of the psychologist and the skill in weighing and interpreting evidence necessary to the historian," Berenson illuminated the whole panorama of Italian painting with his critical writings and attributions, apart from which his monument is the glorious library and art collection he bequeathed to Harvard University. Since his death in 1959 I Tatti has become the Harvard Center for Italian Renaissance Studies. As in the case of Ruskin, there has been a posthumous reaction against him, yet I am not alone in considering his handbooks to Italian painting just as indispensable for students today as when they were published in 1899. Without any panoply of literary pretension his simple statements hit the bull's eye and remain embedded in the memory. The first page of his *Florentine Painters* for instance: "Forget that they were painters, they remain great sculptors; forget that they were sculptors and still they remain architects, poets, and even men of science. They left no form of expression untried, and to none could they say, 'This will perfectly convey my meaning.' Painting, therefore, offers but a partial and not always the most adequate manifestation of their personality, and we feel the artist as greater than his work, and the man as soaring above the artist."

But it was Giorgio Vasari who paved the way for subsequent art historians. His *Lives of the most eminent Painters, Sculptors and Architects* were first published in 1550, to be reissued with additional items in 1568, and in spite of mistakes and chauvinistic prejudices his scheme of the growth of the arts from Cimabue to their culmination in his adored Michelangelo is still valid and enjoyable as literature. Though some of his anecdotes are mythical he depicts his varied characters with a vivid brush. We remember his description of Paolo Uccello as "a shy man ... solitary, strange, melancholy and poor," who "would remain the night long in his study to work out the vanishing points of his perspective" and, when called to bed by his exasperated wife, replied: "Oh, how sweet a thing is this perspective!"

Vasari's biographies of Brunelleschi and Donatello emphasize the originality of their works, based on a study of classical examples. Their visit to Rome enabled them, as Vasari wrote, mentally to reconstruct its grandeur before its fall, and return to Florence to achieve the first consummate masterpieces of Renaissance art.

Donatello revived the portrait bust and the equestrian monument with a difference, instilling his own powerful personality into these creations. Though he had learned the syntax of Roman art, as Sir John Pope-Hennessy wrote, the method by which his free-standing bronze statue of David in the Bargello was constructed had no precedent in the antique: "Donatello when he died in 1466 had developed from the *lingua franca* of Gothic sculpture the language of sculpture as we know it now, had mapped out the future and broken irrevocably with the past, and through unaided intuition had formulated almost all the problems with which later sculptors have been concerned."

Considering Vasari's multifarious activities as painter and architect it is amazing that he collected such a wealth of data for his *Lives*. No painters or sculptors were included among the brief biographies compiled by Vespasiano da Bisticci (1421-1498), the bookseller who helped to form the libraries of Cosimo de' Medici the Elder and Federigo da Montefeltro. Written in the vernacular as rough material for lapidary Latin compositions, these were not published till the nineteenth century. Among popes, kings, and cardinals he wished to commemorate the outstanding scholars and literati of the early fifteenth century when, as he wrote with justifiable pride, "all the seven liberal arts have been fruitful in men of distinction." The desire to perpetuate a name was already more prevalent in Florence than elsewhere, and it produced the noblest monuments in Santa Croce.

The name of the Medici has been perpetuated more extensively than that of any other Florentine family by its leadership in culture and patronage of the arts. Michelangelo, the last and most versatile master of the Renaissance, was a favoured protégé of Lorenzo the Magnificent in his boyhood; the seated statues in their niches and the recumbent figures of Night and Day, Twilight and Dawn, in the new sacristy of San Lorenzo, since familiar as the Medici Chapel, are among the finest plastic expressions of his maturity, elevating him to the level of Shakespeare and Beethoven in poetry and music.

It is a common misapprehension that the arts declined in Florence after Michelangelo's death in 1564, but there was plenty of talent and sporadic genius among the Mannerists who tried to emulate him. Having reached a peak of perfection, Michelangelo's was a difficult heritage which evidently inhibited his successors. Without his spiritual involvement they tried to imitate his strength by the exaggeration of sheer muscle. The contrast between Michelangelo's *David* and the neighbouring *Hercules and Cacus* by Baccio Bandinelli is almost comical, yet the latter was no mean sculptor by modern standards. As for Benvenuto Cellini, surely his *Perseus and Medusa* is a triumph of virile elegance. Giambologna was a Fleming by birth but a Florentine by adoption, and he instilled fresh life into Florentine sculpture when it was in danger of becoming academic. All his best work, the celebrated flying figure of *Mercury, The Rape of the Sabine Women,* and *Samson and the Philistine,* were influenced by the bronzes in the Medici collection. His assistants, Pietro Francavilla, Antonio Susini, and Pietro

Tacca, continued to use his models in the Borgo Pinti studio while inventing new compositions of their own. Dr. Berti's masterly book *Il Principe dello Studiolo: Francesco I dei Medici e la fine del Rinascimento fiorentino* (1967) provides a lucid exposition of this period when Florence had become the capital of an important state under the Medici Grand Dukes.

The sculptors and architects of the seventeenth century were, on the whole, superior to the painters, but to dismiss them as a diminuendo of decadents is absurd, for their fertility of imagination was quite as remarkable as their technical virtuosity. The fine arts flourished as long as the Medici lasted. A demonstration of this was provided in 1974 when two exhibitions called "The Twilight of the Medici" were held in Detroit and in Florence. As a biographer of the last Medici I may be over-partial, but it seems to me that many of these artists are worthy of reappraisal, especially the sculptors Soldani and Foggini. Under the Habsburg-Lorraine Grand Dukes taste became more cosmopolitan, tending towards the Neoclassicism of Canova and his school, but it left even fewer traces than the Baroque.

Ultimately the Renaissance is paramount. Here Aristotle's definition in the *Poetics*, "Beauty lies in bigness of style and in construction," is most frequently exemplified. One is constantly impressed by the wonderful sense of volume conveyed by Tuscan buildings. Whether richly decorated or severely simple, the basic construction is sound. The Florentine instinct for simplicity and harmony – its avoidance of excess – must have been influenced by the surrounding landscape. It is a landscape seldom spectacular but always civilized – the cultivated vineyards and olives providing a delicate tracery against the gently undulating hills. The atmosphere is usually luminous but when it happens to be misty, as Hawthorne noticed, the mist "sets it beyond the limits of actual sense and makes it ideal: it is as if you were dreaming about the valley – as if the valley itself were dreaming, and met you halfway in your dream." And when the church bells ring out you succumb to the timeless enchantment.

Weary of synthetic and standardized products, and of the levelling process of urbanized communities elsewhere, in Florence we may "cultivate our garden" without interference, gratefully recalling that old Greek inscription: "The Healing-place of the Soul."

Sir Harold Acton
Florence 1979

History of the City
and of its Development

Florentia

The medieval Florentines boasted of ancient and noble origins, like the woman in Dante's poem who, while spinning, would tell her children tales of Troy and Rome and Fiesole. Behind these half mythical, half historical fantasies, and behind the assertion that the city was the "daughter" of Rome, there lay, however, a basis of truth. The history of Florence goes back a long way. Even though Homer's Troy may have had nothing to do with it, nevertheless, between the tenth and eighth centuries B.C., there did exist an Italic city of Villanovian culture. The cemetery of this city lay in the present centre of Florence, in the area to the west of Piazza della Repubblica, and a collection of burial urns from it can be seen in the Archaeological Museum. At that time, almost 3000 years ago, the Mugnone, a torrent, flowed into the Arno where the Santa Trinita bridge now stands, and the river-bed upstream seems to have been divided into several shallow branches, offering easy fords and good opportunities for trade. This village must have disappeared when, from the seventh century onward, the land was ruled by the Etruscans who developed small farming settlements. Despite the smallness of these settlements, such a rich and lavishly appointed tomb as the one found at Montagnola di Quinto bears witness to the degree of prosperity and culture they must have reached.

In the fifth century this peaceful rural community was destroyed, probably by a Gallic invasion, and we have no further evidence of Etruscan civilization until the end of the fourth century, with the fortified centre of Fiesole on the hill immediately to the north of Florence. And it was not until 59 B.C., with Caesar, that the site of the ancient Villanovians was reinhabited. A Roman colony, later expanded by Octavian, was founded and given the hopeful name of *Florentia*. It is also possible that it was called Florentia because of the fertility of the surrounding area (arva florentia), or because of the meeting of the rivers (fluentia). The settlement was of a typically Roman design: a square area with sides roughly half a kilometre long: it was located in the present centre of the city. Brick walls, with gates and round turrets, followed the length of the present Via Cerretani and the Cathedral Square at the north, Via del Proconsolo at the east, the northern side of the Palazzo Vecchio at the south, and Via Tornabuoni at the west. The *Cardo maximus*, the main thoroughfare, corresponded roughly to Via Calimala and Via Roma; the *Decumanus maximus*, at right angles to it, was formed by Via Strozzi and Via del Corso. At the crossroads stood the forum (in the present Piazza della Repubblica), with the Temple of the Capitol dedicated to Jupiter, Juno and Minerva, in its western corner. The four sections of the city, formed by the intersection of the *Cardo* and the *Decumanus*, were then subdivided into smaller zones by minor roads. Present-day Florence still retains this chess-board appearance.

Initially Florentia was architecturally very modest, but later it developed a prosperity which was reflected in its buildings, reaching its climax in the second century under the rule of the Emperor Hadrian. The Forum was enlarged in the direction of Via Calzaioli and paved in marble; then it was surrounded by marble buildings and arches. Finally, an aqueduct made the construction of two baths possible, one behind the Capitol and the other to the south, by the walls, in what is now Via delle Terme (Street of the Baths). It became common to pave one's floors with mosaics and inlays and to have marble wainscotting. The growing population brought about the creation of suburbs outside the walls, along the roads; the city expanded especially

*Archeological Museum
Prehistoric urn.*

7

eastwards, along the Arno. A theatre was built on the site of the Palazzo Vecchio; a Temple to Isis in Piazza San Firenze and a large amphitheatre, with a major axis 113 metres long, near Santa Croce. The shape of the latter can still be seen in the curved streets of the area, such as Via Torta (Crooked Street). The prosperity of Florentia was due to agricultural produce, trade and artisanship, such as clothweaving. Also, thanks to her position on the Arno, Florentia could exact dues from those wishing to cross it. But it was the Arno itself which created the first problems for the city: in 16 A.D. the Emperor Tiberius, in order to reduce the disastrous flooding of the Tiber, decided to divert the river Chiana into the Arno. It was only through the continuous pressure exerted by the Florentine ambassadors, as Tacitus tells us, that the edict was finally revoked.

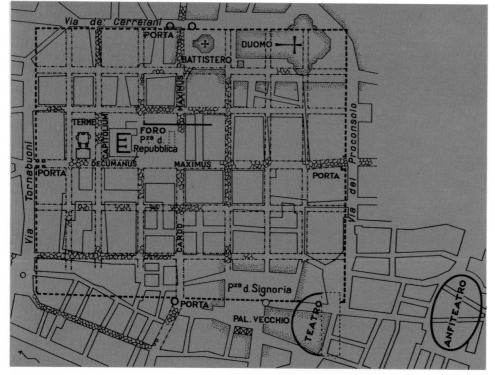

Map of the Roman colony of 'Florentia'.

Christians and Barbarians

In the meantime Christianity had spread to Florence. Towards the year 250 we hear of the first martyr, Miniato. In 313 we hear of a bishop, Felix, who took part in a Roman synod. The new religion had probably been imported by eastern merchants, Greek and Syrian, coming from Rome along the Cassian way. Although along this major road there are many pagan tombs, immediately opposite Florentia, on the other side of the river, catacombs and an early-Christian cemetery have been found. Near the present church of Santa Felicita, sarcophagi and tombstones have been discovered, such as the tombstone in Greek lettering dedicated to a three-year-old girl, dated 417, and one in memory of Paolina Aquila who died in 436.

Cathedral
Santa Reparata excavations.
The altar of the previous
cathedral.

Another early-Christian cemetery has been found near the church of San Lorenzo, just outside the Aquilonare Gate on the north side of the city. San Lorenzo itself, built by a Jewish convert, Giuliana, was consecrated in 393 by St. Ambrose, bishop of Milan and was for a long time the Cathedral of the city. It was here that St. Ambrose gave his sermon "Exhortation to chastity", a text which has come down to us intact. Another early Christian church inside the walls was Santa Reparata (fourth-fifth century) where the Cathedral now is; and also probably the Baptistry, although we are uncertain as to its precise date of construction (sometime between the fifth and seventh centuries).

By this time the Empire was in decline and in 405 the city was besieged by the Ostrogoths. Even though the Florentine general Stilicone was able to defeat them, the damage they had caused to the countryside around the city was enough to bring about the capitulation of Florence to the Goths a few years later. A period of peace ensued, especially under the rule of Theodoric the Goth, but in 541 the city was again besieged and occupied, this time by the troops of the Empire, the Byzantines. This happened during the war against Totila, the king of the Ostrogoths, and the Byzantines barricaded themselves in a small central part of the city, using what was left of the great Roman buildings – the baths, the Capitol and the theatre – as a basis for their fortifications. Then in 570 the Lombards occupied Tuscany, and for the two centuries of their rule the city pursued a course of inexorable and uneventful decline.

Santissimi Apostoli
The interior
(twelfth century).

With the advent of Charlemagne, who visited Florence three times, we find the Lombard duke being replaced initially by a count then by a marquis, ruling over the whole of Tuscany. In 825 the emperor Lothair established in Florence one of the eight Italian ecclesiastical schools. The city, slowly regaining its prestige, enjoyed a position of status under the Ottonian Emperors as well, so much so that Marquis Ugo of Tuscany, who died in 1001, preferred it to the official seat of Lucca. In the meantime the city had grown again to the size of the Roman Florentia, extending as far as the Palazzo d'Altafronte on the Arno, the present Palazzo dei Giudici (Palace of the Judges). The construction of churches continued under all the different rulers: Sant'Apollinare and San Ruffillo belong to the period of the Byzantine occupation; Orsanmichele and San Michele Bertelde (today San Gaetano) were built during the Lombard occupation and are consecrated to the Archangel worshipped by them; San Remigio and Santissimi Apostoli date from the time of the Empire. The worship of St. John the Baptist as the patron saint of the city seems to have begun during the Lombard rule, replacing the worship of Mars.

Medieval Florence

The eleventh century was a period of violent religious strife between a powerful clergy, made richer by virtue of imperial concessions, corrupt and simoniac, and a fiery reformist party led by San Giovanni Gualberto the founder of the Vallombrosa order. Despite all this, ecclesiastical architecture flourished and the great Romanesque churches of Florence belong to this period: San Miniato and the restoration of both the Baptistry and San Lorenzo; San Piero Scheraggio, the harmonious Santissimi Apostoli, Santa Trinita (the crypt of which has remained untouched), San Pier Maggiore (which collapsed in 1783), Santo Stefano al Ponte near the Ponte Vecchio and San Jacopo sopr'Arno.

The twelfth century was, on the other hand, almost entirely taken up with the hard task of conquering the surrounding territories, while internally the city was busy asserting its communal autonomy. Fiesole was destroyed in 1125 and its population was either dispersed or brought in to swell the numbers of Florence; similarly several castles were besieged and their owners were forced either to flee or to accept unfavourable treaties with the city. The growth of the population caused the building of the new city walls, which enclosed a much vaster area: to the north they reached San Lorenzo; to the east, the far side of Santa Croce; to the west, Santa Maria Novella and to the south the city expanded to the other bank of the river. The area of the city was thus practically quadrupled and was no longer divided into four sections but six. The torrent Mugnone had been diverted, so that it now flowed into the Arno at the Ponte Nuovo (where the Ponte alla Carraia now is), which had been built in 1220 as a second bridge; in 1237 the Ponte Rubaconte was added, named after the Milanese Podestà under whose rule it was built, and, in 1252, the Ponte Santa Trinita.

Santo Stefano al Ponte
The facade
(thirteenth century).

The thirteenth century is the century of the schism between Guelphs (supporters of the Papacy) and Ghibellines (supporters of the Empire) and their fierce battles for supremacy. Foreign expansion during this period aimed at the conquest of Siena, as the road to Rome, and of Pisa, as the road to the sea. Yet, despite all this fighting, the city continued to grow and by the beginning of the fourteenth century numbered 105,000 inhabitants. Because of this development a new set of walls was begun in 1248; this was to become a sufficient boundary for Florence until 1865. The walls, with towers and large fortified gates, extended on the right bank of the river as far as the present ring-road and, on the left, from the gate of San Niccolò to the gate of San Frediano. Also in the thirteenth century several impressive churches were built or rebuilt in the new Gothic style: Santa Trinita, the Badia Fiorentina, Santa Maria Maggiore, San Remigio, and above all the grandiose basilicas of Santa Maria Novella and Santa Croce. In the sphere of civic architecture the Palazzo del Podestà, later called the Bargello, was built and the Palazzo di Parte Guelfa, later completed by Brunelleschi, was begun. The Palazzo Vecchio was begun in 1299, at a time when the artisan Guilds were coming to power. The rich aristocracy built themselves towers (more than 150 at this time), but there was also a continuous increase in the number of small shops, yet another sign of the growing prosperity of the artisans and the merchants. The founding of civic institutions, such as the hospital of Santa Maria Nuova, is also of this period.

Santa Maria Maggiore
The facade
(thirteenth century).

The political history of the city from the fourteenth to the seventeenth century will be discussed in detail in another chapter. To conclude the architectural development of Florence during the fourteenth century we must mention that the third set of walls was completed in 1333. This century also witnessed the completion of the Palazzo Vecchio, the extension of the Palazzo del Podestà, the gradual construction of the Cathedral, the continuation of the monasteries of Santa Maria Novella and Santa Croce, the building of Orsanmichele, the Loggia del Bigallo, the Loggia dell'Orcagna and many other religious, civic and private buildings.

The architectural style and design of the private houses, built in clusters

around the palaces of the richer and more powerful families, gave way to more comfortable houses with internal courtyards the ground floor of which was used for commercial and mercantile purposes. The city was by this time industrially very rich, with over 200 workshops of the Wool Guild, producing between 70,000 and 80,000 items every year and employing over 30,000 people. There were also 20 workshops in Calimala (a street still called by this name) which specialized in the treatment of imported materials. The fiscal revenue of the Commune amounted to over 300,000 florins a year. The population explosion had come to a halt even before the dreadful plague of 1348, which wiped out almost two-thirds of the population. Immediately after this catastrophe, in 1349, a body responsible for town planning, the Ufficiali della Torre, was created. The narrow and winding smelly streets were made "amplae et rectae" (wide and straight), and most of the street markets in the centre of the city were closed down.

View of Florence in 1352.

Renaissance Florence

At the beginning of the fourteenth century, although Florence was one of the most important political centres of Italy and undoubtedly its cultural capital, the city only had a population of 60,000. (According to a census taken in the time of Cosimo I, the population had not grown by 1561). The tremendous artistic output of the Renaissance was concentrated more on the renovation of pre-existing buildings than the construction of new ones. In fact, within the somewhat ambitious area enclosed by the fourteenth century walls, there were vast portions of unoccupied land. Brunelleschi's dome, the most impressive undertaking, dominated the entire city; Brunelleschi also rebuilt the basilicas of Santo Spirito and of San Lorenzo. His architecture, which emulated antique architectural principles and styles, was called "modern" to distinguish it from the gothic, or "old" style. This same architect also built the Foundling Hospital of the Innocents for orphans with its magnificent arcade along one side of the piazza della Santissima Annunziata. While Cosimo dei Medici used Michelozzo, a far less ambitious architect, for his palace and for the monastery of San Marco, and while another great architect, the learned Leon Battista Alberti, was working on the facade of Santa Maria Novella, on Santissima Annunziata and on the Rucellai Palace, Brunelleschi was planning a grandiose palace at the foot of the Boboli hill. This palace, the Pitti Palace, was destined to become, once it fell into the hands of the Medici, a truly magnificent court.

There is little point in compiling a list of the buildings of this period (in any case, the main ones will be discussed in later chapters), or in enumerating all the architects, sculptors and painters who occupy a large chapter in the history of world art. It is enough to say that the chronicler Dei, writing in the second half of the fifteenth century, gives the figure of 30 new palaces as being built in Florence between 1450 and 1478 alone; he also tells us of 21 loggias, 138 gardens and more than 50 squares, not to mention the development in the countryside of more than 800 villas. In the sixteenth century the spate of building projects continued, the scale became larger as the style changed first to mannerism, later to classicism as can be seen in the work of Giorgio Vasari and Bartolomeo Ammannati. Cosimo I, with his sons Francesco I and Ferdinand I, gave the city the dignity of a capital, the capital of their Grand Duchy. In this century the two fortresses, Fortezza da Basso and Forte Belvedere, were built, although they were probably intended to protect the Medici from internal revolt rather than foreign invaders. The new Market, the Uffizi, the Vasari Corridor, the Boboli Gardens, the New Sacristy and the Laurentian Library at San Lorenzo (the last two both designed by Michelangelo) – all this, and many modernisations and reconstructions, took place during the sixteenth century. A new facade for the Cathedral was even planned in 1587, which sadly involved the destruction of the previously incomplete one. It was the fifteenth and sixteenth centuries which gave Florence that unique appearance which the tourist comes to discover: the exquisite and mellow shapes which replaced the austerity of the Middle Ages, a taste and style which spread from Florence to the rest of Italy and eventually abroad.

The wild boar of this fountain is familiarly called 'the piglet' (Porcellino); anyone who rubs his nose is supposed to return to Florence.

From the seventeenth century to the present day

It is nowadays becoming more acceptable, and quite justifiably so, to take an interest in the four centuries following after Florence's Golden Age of the Renaissance. This period is by no means empty: until 1859 the city was the capital of a Grand Duchy, ruled by the Medici until 1737 and thereafter by the Lorraine family. The Lorraine dynasty was politically progressive and introduced both ecclesiastical and legal reforms. From 1865 to 1871 Florence was the capital of the new-born Kingdom of Italy.

The main glory of seventeenth-century Florence lay in the development of science on the part of Galileo and the Accademia del Cimento. A sphere of activity in which the practical Florentine mind could still reign supreme. But, economically and politically the city was decaying; artistically, Florence shied away from the extravangances of the Baroque. And, although there are a number of impressive constructions, such as the Cappella dei Principi in San Lorenzo, the facade of San Gaetano in Via Tornabuoni, the Piazza San Firenze, the grandiose Corsini Palace, the Loggia del Grano and the enlargement of the Pitti Palace, there was no Florentine artist of any great note.

In the eighteenth century the Lorraine dynasty, although not such great patrons and collectors as the Medici, revitalised the city by virtue of their capable government. In the sphere of the arts they managed to promote some notable undertakings in the Neo-Classical style, such as the White Room in the Pitti Palace, or the Room of Niobe in the Uffizi and the Villa at Poggio Imperiale.

Peter Leopold of Lorraine also took care to reorganize the Uffizi, founded the science museum at La Specola and the museum attached to the academy of Fine Arts, later to house famous sculptures by Michelangelo. Florence became a favourite city for travelling foreigners, especially the English. By 1766 there were almost 80,000 inhabitants.

Then, in 1799, Florence was involved in the Napoleonic whirlwind, but in September 1814, amidst great popular support, Ferdinand III of Lorraine was reinstated, and was later succeeded by the equally popular Leopold II. During this period Florence was unique in Italy for its tolerance and hospitality. It became the centre of an enlightened and progressive culture, which was centred around the library founded in 1819 by Vieussieux. Great Italian and foreign cultural figures came to Florence to admire its artistic beauties and its cultural freedom: Foscolo, Manzoni, Leopardi, Tommaseo, Chateaubriand, Byron, Shelley, Dumas, Von Platen, etc. During the First War of Italian Independence, in 1848-9, Leopold temporarily left the city in the hands of the revolutionaries, so that, during the Second War of Independence, in 1859, his abdication did not come as a surprise. On April 27th the Grand Duke left the city, which the following year was annexed by plebiscite to the infant Kingdom of Italy.

Science Museum
Galileo's telescope.

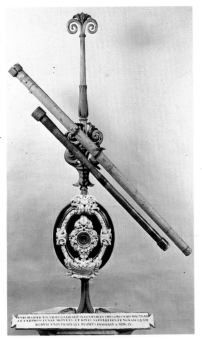

When, a few years later, Florence became the capital of the new state, the sudden growth of the population (to 145,000) called for a large amount of new building and of new planning, undertaken by the architect Giuseppe Poggi. The fourteenth-century walls were demolished and replaced by the wide avenues which surround the city. To the south, the winding Viali dei Colli and the Piazzale Michelangelo were built; the Lungarni (streets along the Arno) and several other streets in the centre were widened, and various residential suburbs were created. The population growth did not stop after the capital was transferred to Rome and now there are about half a million inhabitants. Today Florence has new problems, some perhaps insoluble; but there is no doubt that with its industries, its artisan work, its tourism and its cultural appeal the city has managed to combine its artistic and historical fascination with a modern vitality. Florence has also shown, in the Stadium by Pier Luigi Nervi (1932), the station by Michelucci (1934) and the Church on the Autostrada also by Michelucci, that is has not lost its sense of good taste.

▶

Cathedral
Emilio De Fabris,
the facade (1871-1887).

◀

Cathedral Museum
B. Poccetti (?),
Drawing of the facade of
the Cathedral.

The Religious Centre

*(illustrations
from page 34 to page 56)*

In 1418, applying his scientific method of perspective for the first time. Brunelleschi painted two panels of the Baptistry and of Piazza della Signoria, with a precision which must have seemed almost miraculous. The chioce of the subjects, apart from their interest for linear perspective (he painted the Baptistry frontally, foreshortening two of its sides, and the Palazzo Vecchio at an angle from the distance, in order to give a wide-angle view of the whole square), is not fortuitous: these are the two centres of the city, the one religious and the other civic. Furthermore the Baptistry is an example of classical harmony, serene yet light and colourful with its black and white marble; the Palazzo Vecchio, on the other hand, gives visual evidence of the pride and austerity of the Middle Ages with its powerful and compact mass of brown stone. The two buildings respectively epitomize the gentle, contemplative and spiritual side of Florence and the virile, active and aggressive side. These two fundamental tendencies, these two opposite types of form and expression, were to inspire Brunelleschi himself and the other Renaissance architects.

Yet Brunelleschi could not have attempted to portray the Cathedral Square in its entirety, because it was not a well-defined or compact unit, and we see in the panel only the contours of the Cathedral, the bell-tower and the Baptistry. In the old city maps, in fact, the name of Cathedral Square is restricted to the area enclosed between the Cathedral and the Baptistry, the rest being called Piazza San Giovanni around the Baptistry, and Fondamenti around the Cathedral, because of the large and extremely solid foundations laid by Arnolfo and his successors. But it was here, whether it was called a square or not, that the Florentines met and sat in the warm summer evenings. The bizzarre literary figure A.F. Doni reports a series of dialogues and anecdotes which he calls The Marbles, because they are said to have taken place on the steps of the Cathedral. In one of these dialogues, between the clown Carafulla and a man called Ghetto, a joke is made of the demonstration that the earth moves round the sun, a century before Galileo proved it to be so.

*Codice Rustici
Fifteenth-century Ms.,
the Baptistry.*

The Baptistry

Brunelleschi painted the Baptistry as if seen from the central door of the Cathedral, and also two small areas on either side of it, including the Column of San Zanobi. He had reproduced the Baptistry "with great diligence and gentleness . . . with the colours of the marble." And to give the whole a more realistic touch, he placed on the panel, behind the building itself, not a painted sky, but a sheet of silver which would reflect "the air and the sky . . . and also the clouds . . . moved by the wind." This was the time when the artistic aim of both the Florentine and the Flemish painters was to reproduce accurately all the visual aspects of the world. And if this panel shows a great love of reality, we must not forget that the subject of the painting, the Baptistry, was the great love of Florence. Dante, in his exile, recalls "my beautiful San Giovanni" and the time when he broke a baptismal font to save the life of an infant (Inferno, Canto XIX).

Baptistry
Lorenzo Ghiberti,
Self-portrait
(from the Porta del
Paradiso).

The Florentines loved the Baptistry because it was a sign of their historical importance; it was dedicated to St. John, the patron of the city; and, above all, it was an example of artistic excellence to which all other art must aspire. It was believed to have been built originally as a temple to Mars, during the time of Augustus, and dedicated by the Romans to celebrate the victory over the Etruscans in Fiesole. Spared during the invasion of Totila, it was believed to represent the noble Roman origins of the city, and the perfection of that art before the barbarous medieval styles. Dante makes his ancestor Cacciaguida, in *Paradise*, call it 'ancient', a word which in Florence meant much more than simply "old"; "and in your ancient Baptistry I became both Christian and Cacciaguida." Even the artists of the Renaissance, despite their knowledge of Roman art, considered it ancient. And today the most generally accepted theory is that it was built between the fifth and seventh centuries. We find it mentioned as early as 899, but there must have been a certain amount of Romanesque reconstruction including the marble exterior for it was reconsecrated in 1059 by Pope Nicholas II. Then in the fourteenth century the level of the square was raised, and the steps on which it rested, which had given it a more slender appearance, were lost. In any case, it would seem unlikely that in Dante's time the Florentines did not remember its construction only two centuries before. What is certain is that, with its calculated structure, including the marble exterior, and its lack of superfluous elements, the Florentine Baptistry is far more than a typical example of Romanesque art, usually much cruder and less refined. And even if the eye of the expert can distinguish a light element of rigidity, the decoration, the grace, the sophistication, the *ésprit de géometrie* and the proportions of this building, form the first and basic element of Florentine art. Cinelli, in 1677, was to write: "one can still see how the great Architecture, in use up to this day, was all inspired by this buiding."

National Museum (Bargello)
Filippo Brunelleschi,
Sacrifice of Isaac.

Lorenzo Ghiberti,
Sacrifice of Isaac.
The panels for the
competition (1402).

The Building of the Cathedral

Dante, born in 1265, saw the thirteenth-century mosaics on the vault of the Baptistry almost completed: the gigantic *Christ in Judgment*, the celestial hierarchies of saints and angels, the horrendous scenes of Hell and the torments of the damned, today attributed to Coppo di Marcovaldo. These are visual scenes which may have inspired the writer of the *Divine Comedy*. But the art which he must have felt contemporary and similar to his own was not the sharply archaic art of those mosaics, but the other, more human art which was developing at his time in Florence, the art of Arnolfo di Cambio (born in 1240) and Giotto (born in 1266).

In 1294 the Florentines decided to renew their Cathedral, replacing the old Santa Reparata (built in the fourth or fifth century, some remains of which have recently been uncovered under the floor of the Cathedral) with a larger church which would be able to rival the Cathedrals at Siena and Pisa and which could hold as many as 30,000 people and which, in the words of the decree of the republic, "should possess the utmost and most sumptuous magnificence." As the contemporary chronicler Villani writes, the previous Santa Reparata appeared "crudely built and too small for such a city." A new taste had developed together with the growing political power of Florence and the old buildings were no longer considered magnificent enough. Special taxes, fines and the income from the forests of the Casentino and of Romagna, were allocated to finance the enterprise. When in 1471 at last the gold ball with the Cross was placed on top of the Cathedral, and the clergy had climbed up to sing a *Te Deum* of thanks, 175 years had passed since the first foundations had been laid in 1296, and the total expense had been eighteen million gold florins.

Dante was only able to see the beginnings of the Cathedral, the work of a famous architect, Arnolfo, who had already worked for the king of Sicily and the pope. He saw the gigantic clover-shaped foundations (according to the French model); he saw the beginnings of the work on the facade, for which Arnolfo was sculpting enormous statues (now in the Cathedral Museum); he saw what a document of 1300 called a 'magnificent beginning'. A plaque of the last century, which reads 'Rock of Dante', shows that the poet is traditionally supposed to have been a frequent visitor to the site.

In 1302 Arnolfo died (although recent scholars tend to place the date a little later) and Dante was exiled. Arnolfo's work, which in size and concept can be compared to Dante's monumental poem, was eventually to be finished many years later. The work was resumed after the definitive model had been agreed upon in 1367; in 1375 Santa Reparata, which until that time had been spared by building the outer walls of the new church around it, was demolished; in 1436 Pope Eugene IV was able solemnly to consecrate the Cathedral after the completion of Brunelleschi's dome. A decree of the Signory, threatening severe fines, had dissuaded the Florentines from calling the new church Santa Reparata, a name to which they were accustomed, and to adopt the new name of Santa Maria del Fiore.

Montaigne – who took some time to be convinced of the beauty of Florence – wrote of the Cathedral in 1568 as being merely "enormous . . . one of the richest works in the world"; and Burckhardt in 1855 levelled various criticisms at it, but did recognize that, once inside, "as you gradually enter into the spririt of the construction," one feels "an almost terrifying power." This definition is still one of the most valid, putting across the impression of the visitor, who finds that the eighteen million florins were spent, especially in the interior, not on the creation of outward splendours, but rather to express the idea of a severe and solemn godhead, boundless and eternal.

Codice Rustici Fifteenth-century Ms., the Cathedral.

Giotto's Bell-Tower

It is usually agreed upon that the foremost art in fourteenth-century Florence was that of painting, thanks to Giotto, whose dominant influence was expressed even by Dante in *Purgatorio* when he says that Cimabue's great fame was overshadowed by that of Giotto. And Cennini towards the end of the century was to produce a famous definition of this painter reflecting the general artistic trend of the time: Giotto "changed the art of painting from Greek (Byzantine, oriental) to Latin and made it modern; his art was the most accomplished of anyone's." Giotto had learnt a great deal from Arnolfo's statues originally on the Cathedral facade (now in the Cathedral museum), for instance Arnolfo's two very human and expressive saints adoring the Virgin and Child can be compared to the angels in Giotto's *Ognissanti Madonna* in the Uffizi in their amplitude and serenity.

After Arnolfo's death, work on the Cathedral came to a halt until, in 1334, the aged Giotto was given the post of supervisor to the works. In that same year he began work on the bell-tower, which, but for his death in 1337, might have given us a truly novel and original work. A detail of a fresco of 1352 shows the Baptistry and the facade of the Cathedral begun by Arnolfo, together with the still existing Santa Reparata within it, and the foundations of Giotto's bell-tower. Work on the bell-tower continued with Andrea Pisano and later Francesco Talenti, and was completed in 1387 with a total expense of eleven million florins. It is said that Charles V considered the bell-tower "a precious jewel which should be preserved under a bell-jar." (As we can see the worries about how best to safeguard Florence's artistic heritage started very early.) The bell-tower, as has been pointed out, marks a turning-point in Florence's Gothic architecture. Until this time, in Santa Maria Novella, in Santa Croce, in the interior of the Cathedral, Florentine architecture had been characterised by grand but sobre structures; but now, in the bell-tower the strength of the structure is disguised and the preciousness and pictorial values are emphasised: the marble reliefs, niches, statues and crenellated windows. Perhaps Giotto had envisaged crowning the tower with an ornate gothic spire, but Talenti completed the tower with a horizontal cornice.

Giotto also had a hand in the design of the relief panels around the base of the bell-tower. In the 26 medallions and the 16 statues, a complete story is developed: the creation of man and his discovery of the various arts, both practical and contemplative; the planets which influence life and the virtues and the sacraments which sanctify it; the patriarchs, the prophets and the sibyls. Its basic meaning was the redemption of man, after original sin, through work, moral strength and divine grace concretely applied by the church with its rites. The result was that the scenes were not symbolic or directed towards transcendental life, but illustrated the manifold reality of life and society, making a synthesis of its various activities, according to the principles of Scholasticism. Even though this complex programme was the work of learned ecclesiastical counsellors, it was that which best adapted itself to an industrious city, active rather than contemplative and progressive, such as fourteenth-century Florence; and to a "modern" and "natural" artist such as Giotto. The bas-reliefs are the work of Andrea Pisano, who had already, under the influence of Giotto, created the first bronze door of the Baptistry (1329-36); but Giotto's influence was determining in these sculptures, in giving them an extreme clarity and a representational force, inspired by everyday life.

It is indispensable to see the originals (replaced by copies on the bell-tower, in order to preserve them) in that extraordinary and little-visited museum, the Cathedral Museum. The bas-reliefs here can be admired from close up, and even from the sides, views which on the bell-tower were lost. We will mention only a few: the shepherd in his solitary tent, whose dog keeps watch over the sheep; *Tubalcain* the blacksmith, in his forge with all the tools of the trade; the drunken *Noah* in his grape arbour, with the barrel shown in perspective; *Medicine*, with the doctor who, while his patients wait, is examining a urine sample; *Weaving*, which recalls one of the main Florentine contemporary activities with the purity of a Greek relief; *Daedalus* flying in an empty sky (almost as if the Florentines foresaw that one day flying would be a common activity); the boatmen bending over the oars in *Navigation*; the effort of the oxen drawing the plough in *Agriculture*; the three scenes of the architect, the sculptor and the painter each in his workshop; the horseman riding in the hunt. Among the Planets, a benevolent *Venus* holds a naked couple in the act of love. It has been pointed out that 'this is perhaps the first time since classical antiquity that lovers were portrayed naked.' Among the *Sacraments* the work of A. Arnoldi, we must point out the realism of the elevation of the Host in the *Eucharist*, with the backview of the celebrant. The marble figures stand out from blue backgrounds, some now lost, in a way which foreshadows Luca della Robbia's effective system of representation, with the contrast of white on blue. And in fact, Luca della Robbia, in the following century (1437-9), was to sculpt the last five reliefs, among which are the scene of *Grammar* and that of *Orpheus* making music in the forest with the animals listening on.

Giotto was an artist of bourgeois mentality, above all anxious to establish his name and somewhat avaricious, and, as has been pointed out by a sociological critic (Antal), in his and Andrea Pisano's bell-tower the religious content has been twisted to represent above all productive, bourgeois, lay, profane values, with the introduction of many novelties unknown in earlier cycles. Among the activities, the agricultural ones are no longer dominant as had been the case with the Romanesque cycles of the *Months*; here other activities, those of the city, have taken over, industrial, professional and even genuinely artistic ones. Work is no longer portrayed in its most humble aspects, but has been ennobled, a definite sign of progress. In *Sculpture*, the artist is not working on the statue of saint with flowing robes, but is chiselling a classical nude; in *Hercules and Cacus*, the anatomy of Hercules is exalted by its strength and beauty, as Donatello, Michelangelo and Giambologna were to do later in their "heroic" nudes. Even the series of the *Sacraments* is illustrated by "genre" scenes, like the wedding with its very realistic characters. Whereas in the great Gothic cathedrals the sculpture presented the celestial world as a refined feudal court, in Giotto's bell-tower the theme of the Redemption of man is presented in a coherent system: the complex variety of city life is shown, less aristocratic but no less proud, led by the guilds of the major and minor crafts.

The Baptistry Doors:
Ghiberti and Brunelleschi

Although the Florentine bourgeois society placed great emphasis on competition and the success of the individual, it also favoured collective decisions in matters of great importance. All these traits can be seen at work in the major artistic and architectural undertakings of the fourteenth and fifteenth centuries. The long drawn out construction of Santa Maria del Fiore was punctuated by endless discussions; finally in 1366-7 a competition was held to select a definitive model in which many architects took part as well as the painters Taddeo Gaddi and Andrea Bonaiuti. The latter, in a fresco in Santa Maria Novella, was probably recalling his own project even though it was subsequently modified: the windows in the central aisle are round and not ogival, the flying buttresses on the side naves were eliminated, and the drum beneath the dome was designed by Brunelleschi. But, even though the model which was selected was that proposed by the goldsmiths and the painters, it was the architect Francesco Talenti who played the major role in the construction.

The Guild of Calimala, which financed the works on the Baptistry, also announced a competition in 1401-2 for a new door, to be added to the one by Andrea Pisano. Seven Tuscan artists took part, among whom the great Sienese sculptor Jacopo della Quercia; but the choice was narrowed down to two very young competitors, both 24 years of age: Filippo Brunelleschi and Lorenzo Ghiberti. Their two pieces presented for the competition are today at the Bargello, and illustrate the set theme of the *Sacrifice of Isaac*; the time limit for the preparation of the models had been a year. Brunelleschi executed his very rapidly and without mentioning it to anyone; Ghiberti, on the other hand, worked slowly, continually seeking the advice of experts, whom he expected would be later called upon to judge the entries, destroying and starting again many times, according to the advice he received. The victory went to the latter, who had so ably prepared his ground, and the 34 judges chose Ghiberti's piece unanimously. The judges were perplexed by Brunelleschi's model, which combines learned quotations from antiquity (the figure of the youth extracting a thorn from his foot, or the sheep, an hellenistic motif) with highly realistic elements (like the strong muleteer bending over, giving his mule water) and the dramatic tension of Abraham who is about to cut Isaac's throat, if he were not held by an angel, and the cry of despair coming out of Isaac's mouth. Certainly Ghiberti achieved a more harmonious composition, and by dividing the scene diagonally, he created more space for the figures, both for the two talking bystanders on the left and for the main group of Abraham, Isaac and the angel on the right. Where Brunelleschi tells the tale with the tension of a historian, Ghiberti tells it with lyrical elegance; and, if Brunelleschi expresses himself in a dry, traditionally Tuscan fashion, Ghiberti, in his efforts to win, manages to capture the sophistication of the International Gothic style. His decision is understandable, in that he probably found the Florentine taste of the beginning of the fifteenth century too 'modern'. So Ghiberti was given the task of making the door and carried it out with 'great diligence' (as he himself wrote) over the next twenty years with the help of, among others, Donatello, Paolo Uccello and Michelozzo. His foundry therefore became a school which contributed towards making Florence the most important centre for Renaissance sculpture.

Brunelleschi's revenge came in 1418, with the completion of the construction of the dome of the Cathedral, which has a diameter of 45 metres (approximately 150 feet), which, according to the methods of the time, would have required gigantic wooden frameworks, extremely expensive if not actually unattainable. Ghiberti, thanks to the prestige achieved with his door, was a consultant for the construction of the Cathedral, but the problem required the mind of an engineer and was beyond his abilities. Brunelleschi at first put forward all sorts of seemingly insurmountable difficulties, then proceeded to produce the answers to them. And this time Brunelleschi also worked·cunningly against Ghiberti and his intrigues, finally succeeding in having him removed as his collaborator. (He pretended to be ill, thus placing Ghiberti in the embarrassing position of having to take over the works, for which he had no plan.)

The dome is a technical masterpiece, built with movable scaffolding calculated in every detail, its enormous mass reinforced by marble ribs which exert a powerful centripetal force; it became a focal point, the centre of any view of the city, visible even at a great distance, and overpowering when, seen from close up, against the background of narrow alleyways. Moreover, this gigantic construction places the city on a level with the natural landscape, with the masses of the surrounding hills; this is not only a modern observation, since we can read in Vasari "she reaches such a height, that the hills around Florence seem the same height."

But the dome, the work of the genius of one person and not of collective collaboration, was also the affirmation of Renaissance individuality, and the practical demonstration that man, after the Middle Ages, had been able to regain those supreme abilities possessed in antiquity. Alberti, back from exile, saw the dome in this light and praised it, in 1436, with the following memorable lines: "such a great construction, high above the sky, so large as to protect in its shadow all the Tuscan peoples..." And with these words Alberti was being unconsciously prophetic, because Florence, with the dome as part of the horizon, was already becoming the political capital of Tuscany, as well as the cultural capital of the Renaissance.

In the meantime, Ghiberti, having finished the first Baptistry doors, had obtained the commission for a second, which he was to carry out as he saw fit. He worked on it for 27 years, from 1425 to 1452. In the design of these doors Ghiberti abandoned the Gothic style of the earlier pair and adopted the system of perspective advocated by Brunelleschi, and the pictorial style of Donatello. The scenes are filled with crowds of people ("in some stories I have placed as many as one hundred figures", he wrote), and the ornate Gothic delineation of the forms has been substituted by a clear naturalism. In one scene, Ghiberti returned to the subject-matter of *The Sacrifice of Isaac*, but this time bearing in mind the lesson learnt from Masaccio, Brunelleschi's friend: the naked youth, kneeling and trembling in expectation of the blow, can be compared to those nudes, in the Brancacci Chapel, who are waiting for St. Peter to baptize them. Although he brought to his new door the lessons learnt from other artists, Ghiberti did not forget his own sense of sophisticated and refined harmony, so that still in the sixteenth century this door was considered a perfect work of art: it was Michelangelo who said that it was worthy of being the door to Paradise.

Competition between artists

Some of the masterpieces of Florentine art must be considered in pairs, and in the pair one can contrast two very distinct personalities. In the Cathedral, the *Monument to Sir John Hawkwood* by Paolo Uccello must have seemed spectacular when it was painted in 1436, both because it imitated the classical bronze equestrian monument, and because it reproduced it very simply through the magical illusion of the new system of perspective. A monument done in fresco form was much less espensive and much easier than bronze casting. When Andrea del Castagno in 1456 was given the task of making a frescoed monument of another military leader, *Tolentino*, he used the same scheme as Uccello, but imbued it with a different character; that is, where Uccello had produced a calm and almost abstract atmosphere, Castagno made the whole very energetic. Castagno also replaced Uccello's copper-green horse with one of marble-white. In order to give more emphasis to the brilliance of the rest of the colours; also at the sides of the base there are two putti with coats-of-arms and below a great shell, carefully depicted in perspective. The base is therefore much more full of movement, as is the central group above it: the horse's head is not seen in profile, but turned, creating a play of folds in the skin; the animal's muscular structure is much more detailed; and the saddle ornaments and the rider's cloak are flapping in the wind. Uccello had aimed at reproducing the supreme impassiveness of the monument, whereas Castagno appears to want to return from monumentality to realism.

An even stronger distinction can be seen in the two *Cantorias* (choir lofts), by Luca della Robbia and Donatello. Sculpted for the Cathedral in the 1430's and now in the Cathedral Museum, they are identical in size and of a similar structure (a balcony on five corbels). But Luca della Robbia's young musicians and choristers are poised and composed, whereas Donatello's, against a glittering gold mosaic background, are caught up in a wild dance. Perhaps never as clearly as here, have the two opposite ideals of expression, the *Apollonian* and the *Dionysian*, been placed in such direct contrast. Vasari preferred Donatello's because, in its less refined style, he felt an immediate power, an artistic frenzy; but Vasari's was a taste educated by Michelangelo and the Mannerists and, in any case, he did admit that there were 'talented artists . . . who do not do well except slowly.' But the modern spectator is just as impressed by the purity, the dignity and the intensity of the youths of della Robbia, as he is by the frenzied movement of Donatello's figures.

Contrast and variety characterise the art of fifteenth century Florence, and it was only later with Michelangelo that the dangerous cult of a single personality emerged. Alberti, in 1436, lists five great men of his time: Brunelleschi and Ghiberti, Donatello and Luca della Robbia, and Masaccio; Filarete lists a number of names and Lorenzo the Magnificent commissioned works from a varied group of artists. In 1504, Gaurico, in making a list of Florentine sculptors, mentions as equals, Michelangelo, Andrea Sansovino and Rustici.

The sculptures by Sansovino and Rustici, above the doors of the Baptistry, seem to propose a sculptural alternative to Michelangelo's powerful work. At the time, Michelangelo had just finished the *St. Matthew* now in the Academy, which had been commissioned by the Cathedral Chapter together with the statues of the other eleven apostles. The elegant and precise classicism of the *Baptism of Christ* (1505) by Sansovino is in a certain way almost reminiscent of Ghiberti; it belongs to the same style as Raphael's art. Rustici's *Sermon of John the Baptist* (1506-11), on the other hand, shows the direct influence of Leonardo, Michelangelo's rival, in that the sculptures are very pictorial, with a rich play of light and shadow in the folds of the cloth.

In the Cathedral square, the church of Orsanmichele, the Piazza della Signoria, and in various churches, many works of art, both sculpture and paintings, can be seen which seem to be competing with one another. In order to appreciate them better, they must be compared rather than studied in isolation, just as the artists and the citizens did at the time they were created.

Baptistry
Giovan Francesco Rustici,
The sermon of John the
Baptist
(1506-11).

Andrea Sansovino,
Baptism of Christ (1505).

San Lorenzo,
Chapel of the Princes
Emblem of the city
of Florence.
It seems that originally
it was white on a red
background.
Dante tells us that the
colours were changed for
political reasons.

*Archeological Museum
"Villanovian" urn,
brooch and rasor.
These objects, which bear
witness to the existence of a
civilization before the
Etruscans, were found in the
centre of Florence.*

*Archeological Museum
Mars.
Etruscan statuette of the
sixth century B.C.*

*Archeological Museum
Sarcophagus of
Larthia Seianti.
An interesting
documentation of the life of
the Etruscan ruling class and
of the importance of women
in that society.*

*Cathedral Museum
Roman sarcophagus.*

▶

*Laurentian Library,
"Biadaiolo" manuscript
Florence in the middle ages.
In this manuscript
illumination we can
distinguish the buildings
which have always
characterized the city.*

◄

Santa Maria Novella,
Cappellone degli Spagnoli
Andrea Bonaiuti,
Famous citizens.
It is traditional to identify
the most illustrious
fourteenth-century figures of
the arts in this painting.

Detail of
Giovanni Boccaccio.

Detail of
Giotto and Simone Martini.

Map of Florence
known as the
"Carta della Catena".

►

Church of San Martino
al Vescovo
School of Ghirlandaio,
"Clothe the naked".
A striking example of
everyday Florentine life in
the fifteenth century.

Santa Trinita,
Sassetti Chapel
Domenico Ghirlandaio,
Confirmation of the
Franciscan order.
Two details from this fresco
showing the Palazzo Vecchio
and the Loggia dei Lanzi
in the fifteenth century.

◀

*Filippo Brunelleschi,
Hospital of the Innocents
(Foundling Home).
This is the great architect's
first work in the new
Renaissance style
(1419-1426).*

*Brunelleschi,
Hospital of the Innocents,
internal courtyard.*

*Hospital of the Innocents
Andrea della Robbia, Putto.
The putti on the façade of
the Hospital are the symbol
of this famous institution.*

*Brunelleschi,
Hospital of the Innocents,
Women's courtyard.*

▶

*Palazzo Rucellai.
This palace in
Via della Vigna Nuova
was built by Rossellino
on designs by
Leon Battista Alberti,
and is one of the best
preserved examples of
Renaissance palaces
(1446-1451).*

*Academy of Fine Arts
Master of the
Cassone Adimari,
detail of the Cassone
(wedding chest).
Nearly all Renaissance
palaces had loggias outside,
which were used for
banquets and feasts.*

*Palazzo Vecchio
Giorgio Vasari,
The siege of Florence.
View of the city with its
thirteenth-century walls
during the famous siege by
the Emperor's troops (1530).*

◀
Corsini Palace.
Elegant building built in the
1650s by Pier Francesco
Silvani and Antonio Ferri in
the sobre Florentine Baroque
style.

Santissima Annunziata,
View of the interior.
Seventeenth and
eighteenth-century Baroque.

The Fountain of the
'Porcellino' and the New
Market.
Built by Tasso in 1547, this
loggia now houses the
picturesque straw market.

▶
Art Nouveau house
in Via Scipione Ammirato,
detail of the first floor.

Synagogue.
Built in the late nineteenth
century in Moorish style, it
is the work of Marco Treves
and Vincenzo Micheli.

Church on the Autostrada.
Designed by Giovanni
Michelucci, it is near the
motorway north of Florence.

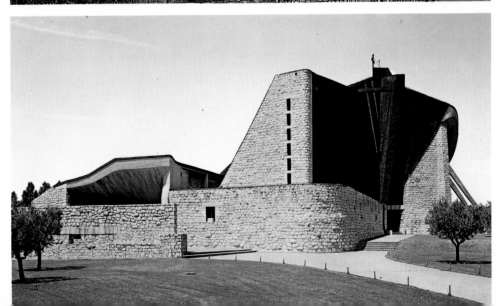

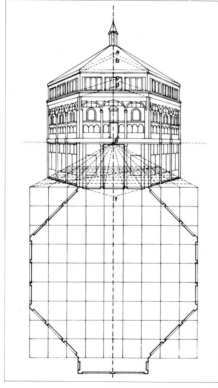

◄
*View of the Cathedral
and the Baptistry.
The religious centre
of the city with its most
distinctive buildings.*

*Baptistry.
It was built on the site of an
early-Christian building;
its coloured marble facing is
typical of Florentine
Romanesque architecture of
the eleventh and twelfth
centuries.*

*Reconstruction of
Brunelleschi's perspective
painting of the Baptistry.*

*View of the inside
of the Baptistry.*

*National Museum
(Bargello)
Rossello di Iacopo Franchi,
the Baptistry at the
beginning of the fifteenth
century.*

►
*Baptistry.
Thirteenth-century mosaic of
St. John the Baptist,
patron saint of Florence.*

*Baptistry
General view of the interior,
with Christ in Judgment
(thirteenth-century mosaic)
and the tomb of
the anti-Pope John XXIII
by Donatello and
Michelozzo.
In the foreground,
Ghiberti's famous
golden doors.*

Baptistry
The vault mosaics.
This cycle, carried out by
many different thirteenth
century artists, marked the
beginning of the Florentine
school of painting.

▶
Two details of the mosaics
on the vault of the
Baptistry:
Hell and the Journey of the
Magi.

Baptistry
Andrea Pisano, South Door.
This was the first of the three doors and dates from the 1330s.

Two details from Andrea Pisano's door: The Baptism of Christ and the Funeral of John the Baptist.

Lorenzo Ghiberti, North Door.
Some details of the second Baptistry door: the Annunciation, a man's head from the decorative framework, a female head and the Adoration of the Magi.

◄

Baptistry
Lorenzo Ghiberti,
East Door,
"Porta del Paradiso".
The most famous of the
Baptistry's three doors,
carried out by Ghiberti
between 1425 and 1452.

A squirrel and a female
figure, part of the
decorative
framework of the door.

Creation of Adam and Eve,
Original Sin, the Fall. ·
First panel.

Adam and Eve at work,
Cain and Abel perform
sacrifices,
Killing of Abel,
Damnation of Cain.
Second panel.

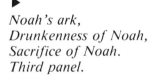

►

Noah's ark,
Drunkenness of Noah,
Sacrifice of Noah.
Third panel.

Three angels appearing
to Abraham,
Sacrifice of Isaac.
Fourth panel.

Stories of Esau and Jacob.
Fifth panel.

Stories of Joseph.
Sixth panel.

Stories of Moses.
Seventh panel.

Stories of Joshua.
Eighth panel.

Stories of David.
Ninth panel.

Solomon and the
Queen of Sheba.
Tenth panel.

◄
*Southern side
of the Cathedral.
This part of the Cathedral,
near the Porta dei Canonici
still retains its typically
Florentine Romanesque
colour scheme.*

*Apse of the Cathedral.
Details of the exedrae,
whose function is
purely decorative.*

*Apse of the Cathedral.
The capitals of one
of the exedrae.*

*Filippo Brunelleschi,
the dome of the Cathedral.
The lantern, which tops
the dome, was built
on designs by Brunelleschi
in 1461.*

►

*Filippo Brunelleschi,
the dome of the Cathedral.
View of the white marble
ribbing, looking down from
the lantern.*

Previous pages:
Filippo Brunelleschi,
the dome of the Cathedral.
Built by the Florentine
architect between 1419 and
1436, it is his most famous
work and the most typical of
Florentine buildings.

Cathedral, interior.
Begun according to a project
by Arnolfo di Cambio
(1296), it was completed on
designs by Francesco Talenti.

Cathedral
Domenico di Michelino,
Dante and the Divine
Comedy.
This painting dates from
1465 and shows the city and
the Cathedral as they were
just after the middle of the
fifteenth century.

Cathedral
Andrea del Castagno,
Monument to
Niccolò da Tolentino. 1456.

Cathedral
Paolo Uccello,
Monument to
Giovanni Acuto
(John Hawkwood). 1436.

*Cathedral
Paolo Uccello,
Clock on the inner façade.
This clock, which dates from
1443, has recently been
restored.*

*Cathedral
Interior of the dome.
The inside of Brunelleschi's
dome was frescoed with
scenes of the Last Judgment
by Giorgio Vasari,
Taddeo Zuccari and others,
between 1572 and 1579.*

*Cathedral
Michelangelo Buonarroti,
Pietà.
One of the last works
of the great sculptor,
finished after his death
by his pupil Tiberio
Calcagni.*

Siena,
Cathedral Museum
Drawing for the bell-tower
of the Cathedral of Florence.

Bell-tower
The Florentine bell-tower
was begun by Giotto,
continued by Andrea Pisano
and finished by
Francesco Talenti and
Neri di Fioravanti
(after 1348).

Lower part of the bell-tower.
The colour scheme of the
marble facing of the
Baptistry and of the
Cathedral
was repeated here too.

► Andrea Pisano
and Alberto Arnoldi,
Venus,
Grammar and the Eucharist.
These are three of the
panels,
dating from different
periods,
which formed the decoration
of the bell-tower.

Luca della Robbia,
Grammar.

Andrea Pisano,
Music,
Navigation and Agriculture.
These panels are among the
oldest and the most
interesting of all those
carried out for the
bell-tower.

◄ *Cathedral Museum Donatello, two details from the Cantoria (choirloft). Donatello's Cantoria, which used to be inside the Cathedral, is characterized by a group of wild boys, running about in a frenetic way.*

▶ *Luca della Robbia, three details from the Cantoria. Youths playing musical instruments, dancing and singing in a choir are the protagonists of Luca's beautiful masterpiece.*

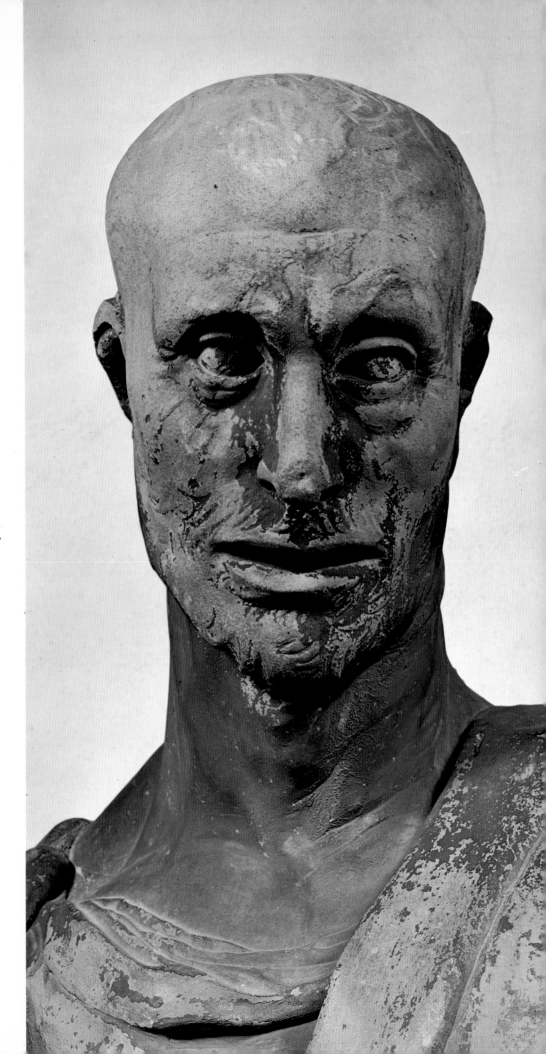

Cathedral Museum

*Donatello,
the prophet Jeremiah.
This figure, a mixture of
Donatello's energetic art
and classical composure,
used to
be in a niche in the
bell-tower.*

*Donatello, Mary Magdalen.
One of Donatello's later
works, this statue has
recently been restored.*

►

*Donatello,
the prophet Habakkuk
(detail).
Popularly called "Zuccone"
(literally "big bald head")
this statue shows all the
realistic strength of the
sculptor.*

Cathedral Museum
Arnolfo di Cambio,
Madonna.
This statue, originally on the façade of the Cathedral, clearly shows the influence of classical art.

Arnolfo di Cambio,
Seated Madonna (detail).
This statue used to be on the central door of the façade of the Cathedral.

(illustrations
from page 73 to page 96)

The Civic Centre

The political system of medieval Florence appears to modern historians complex and ambiguous; for those who lived under it, it was unstable and almost continually in crisis. In theory the city was not independent because of its official submission to the Holy Roman Empire (for example in 1355 it had to pay the emperor, Charles IV, 100,000 florins); but early on Florence joined the anti-Imperial party, the Guelph League, which swore allegiance to the Pope, and thereafter the city fought fiercely against the rival Ghibelline faction (the party of the Holy Roman Emperor). Later on the Guelphs divided into two factions; the Blacks, the conservative element formed by members of the traditionally wealthy classes, and the Whites, the newly rich landlords from the country, who eventually joined the Ghibellines.

The Florentine State did not have total control of all its citizens; the clergy had their own independent legal system and were beyond the reach of the civil law. The aristocracy's power was being slowly curtailed by legal restrictions and their place in society being taken on by the merchant class, but the city still needed them on certain occasions; in time of war they could provide trained knights and soldiers, and they also served as ambassadors and governors of newly conquered territory. An historian has very wittily said that the aristocracy was 'like some poisons, for external use only'. Democracy in the city was very much a relative concept: of a population of almost 100,000, less than 20,000 enjoyed political rights and of those no more than a few thousand members of oligarchical groups could be elected to governmental offices. The poor had no voice in the government and, in 1330, 12% of the population lived on charity. Political feuds were fought by fair means or foul; noble families could be forced to pay exorbitant fines, or even sent into exile. The Palazzo di Parte Guelfa was the courthouse for political inquisition. The period of office was very short, and most officers were elected by the drawing of lots. Thus the executive had no continuity or homogeneity, and was sometimes composed of men who had perhaps been enemies of each other's families for generations, some experienced in government, others who had never been beyond the city walls.

Despite all this, patriotic fervour ran high and the Commune survived internal and external threats. In 1260 the city came very close to being destroyed by the Ghibellines after their victory in the Battle of Montaperti; but by 1267 the city was again securely in the hands of the Guelphs. In 1289 the Battle of Campaldino against Arezzo was won and in 1293 the 'Ordinances of Justice', the basis of the Florentine constitution, were dawn up, whereby the government was placed in the hands of the Priors and the Gonfaloniere of Justice, and the Guilds were made the representatives of the artisans. In 1342 Florence was taken over by a tyrant, the Duke of Athens; however, the following year he was expelled by the Florentines. Pistoia was placed under a protectorate in 1329; Arezzo was bought in 1384 for 40,000 gold florins; Pisa was subjugated in 1406. Thus Florence dominated the entire Arno valley, although during these years it had to contend with many other problems, both internal and external: the war against Pope Gregory XI, 1375-78; the Ciompi revolt of 1378, in which the Florentine citizens called themselves proudly 'the people of God', and the siege of the city by Galeazzo Visconti, the Lord of Milan, who having conquered Pisa, Siena, Perugia, and Bologna appeared to be about to suffocate Florence; but fortunately he died in 1402 before taking the city. The fifteenth century saw the first oligarchy, led by the Albizzi family, which introduced the first great tax reform in 1427. Then followed a decisive struggle between the oligarchy and the Medici, supporters of the people's cause. This resulted in Cosimo the Elder's exile in 1433, but he returned the following year and took control of the government of the city.

During the following century the Medici succeeded in gaining complete control over the city, despite a long period of resistance against them from

Codice Squarcialupi Fifteenth-century Ms., The Captain's Oath.

57

1494 to 1530. Cosimo I was given the title of Duke, and that of Grand Duke in 1569, having conquered Siena in 1555. Apart from Lucca, Florence now ruled over the whole of Tuscany; and Cosimo I governed the region with an iron hand. A chronicler of the late fourteenth century, Marchionne di Coppo Stefani, a good Guelph and a good republican, had already expressed his doubts about the advantage of a more democratic system of government in the city: 'One lord who is alone in his decisions can run a State better than a Commune where there are many men making decisions . . .' It is difficult to say whether the people of Florence were happier during the fourteenth, the fifteenth or the sixteenth century; but it is unquestionable that over these 300 years Florence experienced an extraordinary number of different forms of government. All three centuries achieved some kind of political success, but the city was perhaps never so fully alive or so entirely original as during the unruly years of the fourteenth century, despite the fact that during this time Dante was exiled for his theological beliefs, and Cinto Brandini, a proletarian worker, was hanged in 1345 for having expressed ideas at public meetings held near Santa Croce which were considered dangerous to the citizens' prosperity and to the peace of Florence.

The statute of the Mint.

Palazzo Vecchio

In 1299 the foundations were laid for a palace which was to be the seat of the Priors of the Guilds and of the Gonfaloniere of Justice, the major governing bodies of Florence. The site which was chosen was near the river and next to the old church of San Piero Scheraggio, and the land was bought from some private citizens. The space which was to form the square in front of the palace had once been the site of the houses of the Uberti family, rebels and Ghibellines; this space was therefore damned and never to be built on again. Because of this the building had to be built slightly irregularly and too close to the church. Unlike the Cathedral, the palace was built fairly quickly, probably based on a plan by the architect Arnolfo di Cambio; by 1310 the tower was almost finished, long before Giotto's bell-tower and more than a century before the dome of the Cathedral. Despite the heaviness of the stone and its size, it is nevertheless an elegant building. The ground floor is shut off from the outside, and its only windows are high and barred; the other two floors have elegantly shaped mullioned windows with marble decoration. Above this rises a crenellated gallery and the base of the tower, surmounted by another gallery and more crenellations, culminating in a large belfry. From here the view is phenomenal, encompassing the whole city.

In 1323, an 'aringhiera' was planned along the front and the north side of the palace: this consisted of three rows of seats set against the walls, surrounded by a parapet. The Signoria sat here during official functions. Statues of seated lions holding the emblem of the lily, known as the Marzocco, the symbol of the city, decorated the 'aringhiera'; a pair of real lions was also kept in a cage next to the church of San Piero Scheraggio, which was later to be incorporated into the Uffizi. In July 1331 a lioness gave birth to two cubs, and this was considered a propitious omen for the city. During the two months of their office, the Signoria, which consisted of the Priors and the Gonfaloniere, (which gave its name to the palace and square), had to live, eat and sleep together, almost like cardinals in conclave, to assuage the people's suspicions. It was forbidden to leave the palace except on official business with other members, or to attend the funeral of one's wife

Bayonne, Musée Bonnat
Leonardo da Vinci,
The hanging of Bernardo
Baroncelli after the Pazzi
Conspiracy (1478).

or children; and it was absolutely forbidden to receive women in the palace. They lived on the second floor, all in one room, and were waited on by pages, scribes and ushers. All their armour and official regalia was kept on the ground floor in the Camera dell'Arme.

Palazzo Vecchio was the centre of the city's political life, and it witnessed many political events, many of them stormy, a few peaceful. The Duke of Athens fortified it, stealing materials which were intended for the Ponte Vecchio; but even so, he managed to rule the city for less than a year, and on July 26th 1343, on St. Anne's day, the revolt started. After a brief resistance, the Duke was thrown out of the palace, and some of his supporters were literally torn to pieces. The following year, the Campana del Popolo, the bell of the people, was installed in the belfry, which could be heard throughout the city. In 1378 there was the proletarian revolution of the Ciompi: on 19th July, Bugigatto was tortured by the Signoria in the palace in an attempt to discover the plans of the revolt, but two days later the populace had taken over the palace and Michele di Lando, a wool worker, was made Gonfaloniere. But once in power he suppressed the more extremist members of the Ciompi and, by 1382, the oligarchy was back in power.

From the late fourteenth century a series of eminent men of letters had been installed as chancellor of the Florentine Republic, the first being Coluccio Salutati in 1375, and the governing body in the palace was now combining political experience with intellectual acumen, culture and formal elegance. The enemies of the city recognized the importance of the intellectual weapons of the Florentines, perhaps fearing them more than their armies. Palazzo Vecchio was compared to the Admiral's ship in a fleet, central to all manoeuvres. During the following century, Salutati was succeeded by Leonardo Bruni, Carlo Marsuppini, Poggio Bracciolini, and others who have passed into the history of Italain letters.

In 1433 Cosimo the Elder was called to the palace, arrested and locked in the Alberghettino, or 'Barberia', a small room in the tower. His life was in danger, and he only ate a small amount of bread for fear of being poisoned. He was given two guardians, one of whom, known as Il Fargagnaccio, was renowned for his wit and pleasant conversation and his function was to amuse the prisoner. But with the help of money and friends, Cosimo managed to buy his way out of imprisonment, and had the punishment converted to exile. After his return the following year, the true centre of power in the city passed from Palazzo Vecchio to the Medici's own palace.

During the fifteenth century the Palazzo Vecchio was adorned with works of art, some of which were commissioned, some requisitioned: these included Donatello's *David*, now in the Bargello; an *Adoration of the Magi*, which has disappeared, by the mysterious painter Pesello; paintings by Fra Filippi Lippi, tapestries by Lieven Gillise of Bruges; a bronze *David* also by Verrocchio, now in the Bargello; a fresco by Ghirlandaio; an altar panel by Filippino Lippi now in the Uffizi. But still bloody events continued to plague this building. In 1461 Baldaccio d'Anghiari, the brave captain of the Florentine army, was thrown out of a window and decapitated on orders from the Gonfaloniere; in 1478, after the failure of the Pazzi conspiracy against the Medici, the conspirators, including the Archbishop of Pisa, were hanged from the windows of the palace. In 1498, Savonarola, after his period of ruling the city, during which he had a new hall built in the palace to accommodate the almost two thousand members of his Council, was arrested, locked up in the Alberghettino, tortured and finally hanged and burnt at the stake in the square in front of the palace. The following year, from a torch-lit window in the gallery, the head of Paolo Vitelli, the commander of the militia, who was accused of having treasonably lifted the siege of Pisa, was exhibited to the citizens.

In 1502 Pier Soderini was elected Gonfaloniere for life, and for the first time the palace was inhabited by a woman, his wife Argentina, the daughter of the Marquis of Malaspina. Miniature gardens were created for her, probably in the gallery, which must have softened this severe building.

Soderini also commissioned works of art, such a Leonardo's *Battle of Anghiari*, and Michelangelo's *Battle of Cascina* (only the cartoon, or full size drawing for the composition, was completed); these were intended to be frescoes for the Hall of the Council but sadly nothing is left of them today. And in 1504 Michelangelo's *David* was placed on the 'aringhiera', replacing Donatello's *Judith*, which people were beginning to think brought bad luck to Florence. In 1512, Soderini in his turn was expelled from Florence, (one of his more important advisors had been Machiavelli) and the Medici returned: the Hall of the Democratic Council was taken over by foreign troops as their dormitory. They destroyed the elegant furnishings of the room, which in the words of a contemporary 'displeased the whole city, not so much for the change of government, but for the loss of the beautiful and expensive woodwork.'

On April 26th 1527 the first anti-Medici revolt took place; an illustrious casualty was Michelangelo's *David*, for a stone was thrown down by the defenders of the palace and broke the statue's left arm in three places. It was not repaired until 1543. On May 27th of the same year, the Medici were exiled and the Council reinstated in its old hall; the Republic of Florence was now in its last act. Christ was proclaimed King of Florence, and there is an inscription above the door of the palace to this effect: but this was not enough to save the city from being besieged by troops of the Empire and of the Papacy. After the Republic's surrender, the palace was occupied by the soldiers of Alessandro Vitelli, the son of Paolo, who had been executed in the palace in 1459. In 1532 Alessandro dei Medici was proclaimed Duke and absolute rule of the city, and the Signoria was abolished: one of Alessandro's first actions was to destroy the great bell, which in the democracy had been used to call the entire population together.

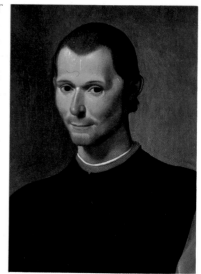

*Palazzo Vecchio
Santi di Tito,
Portrait of
Niccolò Machiavelli.*

*Palazzo Vecchio and
Piazza della Signoria.*

*Siena, Biblioteca Comunale
The Battle of Monteaperti
(1260).*

Cosimo I dei Medici

When Alessandro was assassinated in 1537, the Medici supporters, who were in a minority in the city, feared a rebellion; but the city did not revolt, and a Medici from another branch of the family was found to take over. The Latin 'uno avulso non deficit alter', accompanied by a laurel which, when cut, blossoms from another branch, was a Medici motto. Cosimo, who was only seventeen years old, appeared to be a serious youth, and it was generally thought in Florence that he should be made 'head of the government' but it was assumed that he would be controlled to a great extent by the semi-democratic councils such as the Senate and the Council of the Two Hundred. He was to receive a large allowance and to be given the chance to enjoy himself. Guicciardini, the politician, who was one of the major supporters of this idea, was greatly mistaken in this case: Cosimo revealed himself very early on as a dictatorial ruler. Guicciardini, who had even hoped that Cosimo would marry one of his daughters was embittered by Cosimo's assumption of power, retired to one of his country villas, in political exile, and wrote his monumental *History of Italy*. Mistakes were made by other opponents of the dictatorship, such as Filippo Strozzi, who with some other exiles staged a coup but was discovered and captured. At the beginning of August 1537 a block was placed in Piazza della Signoria where 'for four consecutive days every morning the head of one of the four traitors was chopped off. Filippo Strozzi, initially spared from execution, died the following year, either by suicide or murder, in the Fortezza da Basso, which he himself had partly paid for. After this latest bloodshed, however, the recurrent upheavals in Florentine politics ceased, and a regime which was to last for centuries was installed. The Republic, finally and completely destroyed, had been succeeded by a Principality.

Giambologna, Equestrian statue of Cosimo I.

In 1540, Cosimo and his wife Eleonora, the daughter of the Viceroy of Naples, moved into the Palazzo Vecchio. In the portraits by Bronzino we see the young duke, looking powerful and austere, and his wife Eleonora, ever active and gay, who gave him eleven children, each in turn portrayed by Bronzino. Cosimo was healthy and active, and of an exceptional political ability, which surprised his contemporaries; and although he was not really a man of culture, he did follow in the Medici tradition as a generous patron of the arts. In Palazzo Vecchio he started an impressive programme of building and decorating, at first under the guidance of the architect Tasso and later, after 1555, with the architect and painter Vasari. The new Quartiere degli Elementi was created on Via della Ninna; the Medicean tapestry collection was organised in 1546 to decorate the halls; Bronzino frescoed the Chapel of the Duchess and Salviati the Chamber of Audience. Cellini and Ammannati, who sculpted a fountain for the Great Hall (today the statues are in the Bargello), also worked in the palace. And Vasari celebrated the Medici family with frescoes in all the rooms which had been restored and modernized. The Hall of Five Hundred, which had become the Hall for the duke's audiences, had its ceiling raised and was redecorated by Vasari's workmen: the three main scenes on the left hand wall tell the story of the war for the conquest of Pisa, fought by the popular government, which lasted fourteen years; those on the right, that of the war for the conquest of Siena, undertaken by Cosimo himself which lasted fourteen months. Then in 1565, Michelangelo's heirs gave the duke the statue of *Victory* which was placed in this hall. Here, on the first floor, Cosimo had his private apartments; his mother, his wife and his children lived on the floor above.

It is important to notice that even amidst this great fervour for redecorating the palace, the exterior remained unchanged. Giuliano di Baccio d'Agnolo had presented a project for rebuilding the exterior modelled on Palladio's Basilica at Vicenza. But Cosimo and Vasari saw the outside of the building as a reflection of the old Florence, of the past history of the city, which must be respected; thus it was only the interior that was restored.

When at the end of 1565, Joan of Austria, the daughter of the Emperor and the wife of the Medici Crown Prince Francesco, came to Florence as a bride, the palace had been completely transformed during the previous ten years, and the courtyard had been decorated with views of Austrian cities. The wedding banquet took place in the Great Hall, where the story of Cupid and Psyche was acted; later these Medici theatrical presentations were to be given a special room in the Uffizi. In 1570, near the Hall of the Five Hundred, a study, the Studiolo, was built for the Prince Regent Francesco, who dabbled in alchemy.

Palazzo Vecchio from Cosimo to the present day

Siena had been conquered, thus doubling the size of the State, the organization of the State had been modernized and consolidated, like the Palazzo Vecchio; Florentine political influences were felt everywhere; and yet, perhaps after these tremendous exertions, the duke himself was weakening and growing prematurely old. In 1562, the tragic death of his wife Eleonora and of his children Giovanni and Grazia, who all died of malaria contracted in the marshes of Maremma on a hunting expedition, dealt Cosimo a hard blow. Two years later, to everyone's amazement, Cosimo passed the Regency to his son Francesco, retaining for himself only the ultimate right of veto, and retired to Palazzo Pitti; then he began to have a series of young mistresses, and in 1566, giving signs of having lost the balance which had so characterized his early life, he ordered the murder of his friend Sforza Almeni, whom he accused of having revealed his affair with the young Albizzi girl. In 1568 he had his first cerebral haemorrage; after having been created Grand Duke in 1570, his health got progressively worse, until he was eventually no more than a vegetable, who could neither move nor speak, and in 1574, at the age of 54, he died.

From 1550, the year when Cosimo transferred his court to the palace, primarily for reasons of Eleonora's health, it had become known as Palazzo Vecchio (previously it had been called Palazzo di Sua Eccellenza). In 1588 Francesco's successor, his brother Ferdinand, had commissioned Buontalenti's rear facade; but by the time this was being completed, the palace was no longer really the centre of political life in the city, although it remained the official seat of the government.

In 1801 General Murat installed the government of the Kindom of Etruria in the palace, which in 1807 was replaced by the more direct rule of the Napoleonic Empire with the first mayor of the city; the architect Del Rosso completed some work of restoration, and· removed the historic 'aringhiera'. In 1848 the building was the seat of the provisional government of Tuscany, and from 1865 to 1871 it housed the Italian Parliament, before the capital was moved to Rome; from 1872 it passed into the hands of the Commune of Florence, which has since cared for its upkeep and restoration. This palace has welcomed such famous historical figures as Mazzini and Garibaldi, Cavour and Victor Emmanuel II, Hitler and Mussolini (during their visit to Florence in 1938); and since the war, amidst the political complexities of a democratic Italy, there have been mayors of the international reputation such as La Pira, 'the holy mayor', and Bargellini, 'the mayor of the flood'.

Nineteenth-century patriotic demonstration in favour of Italian unity in Piazza della Signoria.

Piazza della Signoria

Not only is the definitive appearance of the interior of Palazzo Vecchio chiefly due to Cosimo, he is also responsible for the appearance of the square in which it stands, the main square in Florence. During the fourteenth century the square (which, as we have already mentioned, was created by the demolition of the houses of the traitors, the Uberti family) had been a site for the works on the Palazzo Vecchio and the Loggia. It was enlarged on several occasions by the demolition of other houses. Despite the mess caused by the work, the Signory would meet on the 'aringhiera' in front of the palace for important occasions, such as declarations of war, proclamations of peace and alliances, the reception of ambassadors, review of the troops, etc . . . But since the 'aringhiera' was exposed to the elements, following a particularly rainy season in 1374, when all public ceremonies had to be suspended, it was decided that a *loggia* should be built. The Loggia dei Lanzi near the palace, with its three gigantic archways, was built between 1376 and 1382 by the architects Benci di Cione and Simone Talenti. Vasari mistakenly attributed it to Orcagna and it is for this reason that it is still popularly referred to as the Loggia of Orcagna. This loggia is comparable in size more to the ancient Roman monuments than anything else built at that time in Florence.

In 1386 the square was paved in brick, in a herringbone pattern: this can be observed in several paintings, including the two depicting the execution of Savonarola, one of which is now in the Museum of San Marco. This paving was restored in 1507 and lasted throughout the eighteenth century. After the flood of 1966, it was suggested that it should be reinstalled, but nothing came of it. This is a pity because there can be no doubt that this reddish chessboard pattern gave colour and geometric unity to the square, much more so than the present flagstone paving. Everything else about the square is in fact rather irregular, both its shape and the buildings around it. Opposite the Palazzo Vecchio, where there is now an ugly building in fake fifteenth-century style (built in 1871), there used to be the church of Santa Cecilia and another loggia, called the Loggia of the Pisans because it was built by two thousand Pisan prisoners of war in 1364. Opposite the Loggia of Orcagna or Loggia dei Lanzi there is the lovely Palazzo Uguccioni, built in 1550, the facade of which badly needs restoration. On the same side, further down, is the Palazzo della Mercanzia built in 1359, which used to be the courthouse for all mercantile or commercial disputes among Florentine merchants. In the fourteenth century it also housed the headquarters of a public postal service. Several buildings once on the square have been destroyed including the headquarters of the Guild of Calimala (the wool merchants' guild), the palace of the magistrates in charge of agricultural produce, and the church of San Romolo, which was destroyed in 1786.

Cosimo I expressed the wish that the order and unity which he had brought into the political system of the city should be reflected by a unity of architecture. We see the result of this desire, not always felicitous, in the work he commissioned from Vasari in the churches of Santa Croce and Santa Maria Novella. For the square, however, he consulted Michelangelo, who put forward a scheme involving the continuation of the arches of the loggia (which was by now known as the Loggia dei Lanzi, the name of Cosimo's soldiers) around the entire square. This project would have been too expensive and the duke turned it down. Nevertheless during the second half of the sixteenth century the appearance of the square changed considerably. Many statues and works of art were placed in the loggia and in other parts of the square, making it look rather like an open-air museum. Bocchi's guide-book of 1591 says that this square is memorable above all other places in Florence because of its collection of statues. The statues placed in the loggia changed the focal point of the square, so that if one looks into the square from Via dei Cerchi, which runs parallel to the main facade of the Palazzo Vecchio, one's eye is drawn to the loggia. This new viewpoint for the square was shown in an engraving of 1583.

The statues in the square

The first statue one sees from this viewpoint is the *Equestrian Monument of Cosimo I*, by Giambologna, finished in 1598. The bas-reliefs at its base, and especially the one representing *Cosimo's Entrance into Siena*, inspired Rubens who saw them during his visit to Florence in 1600. This monument was however the last to be placed in the square in the sixteenth century. Behind this we see the *Fountain of Neptune* by Ammannati, finished in 1575. This fountain probably was meant to celebrate Cosimo's maritime successes (in fact, Neptune does bear a resemblance to the duke): but it is not the colossal and rather clumsy figure of the god, whom the Florentines rather wickedly call 'Il Biancone', 'the big white one' which attracts one's interest, as much as the purely decorative figures around the base. Some of these sea gods and goddesses, with their stylized elongated bodies, are mannerist in style; but the satyrs, vital and full of movement, are naturalistic in a warm and sensual way. When the old Ammannati, a few years later, was seized by religious scruples under the influence of the Counter-Reformation, he apparently repented having filled his fountain with 'so many nudes', and even begged Cosimo to have them removed, fearing — he wrote — 'that people might think Florence a nest of idols, or of libidinous things'. It is true that by this time Ammannati was considered very pious, but also, according to Borghini in 1583, 'not very right in the head'.

The next statues are those lined along the steps of the palace, where the "aringhiera" used to be. The *Marzocco*, the heraldic lion of Florence, is only a copy of Donatello's original, today in the Bargello. The *Judith and Holophernes*, also by Donatello is an original, but perhaps it would be wise to remove it, to protect it both from bad weather and from the pigeons in the square. It would not be the first time this bronze has been moved; sculpted in 1456, it was suspected of bringing bad luck to the city, because "Judith is a sign of death . . . and it is not right that a woman should kill a man", and it was substituted by Michelangelo's *David*. So the statue was moved first into Palazzo Vecchio, then into the loggia, and was finally placed here, next to the *Marzocco*, in 1919.

The contrast between Donatello's statue and that of Michelangelo which replaced it is immediately apparent: the former is tragic, Judith lifts her scimitar to cut off the head of the dead Holophernes; whereas the *David* is of colossal dimensions, with a calm but titanic strength, expressing the new atmosphere of the sixteenth century. This figure, almost four and a half metres high, is a paragon of beauty and strength, rather like a synthesis of Apollo and Hercules; the Romantics pointed out that this is the turning point in Michelangelo's art, from the "sweet" to the "terrible", although here the two manage to co-exist. This is because of the exaggerated size of this adolescent, strong but slim, calm but ready to fight. In 1873 the original was placed in the Academy and this statue is a copy. It is, however, necessary to look at this copy, where it stands, to form an idea of what the original impression was: in front of the enormous palace and in the open space of the square, the *David* must have looked quite different. It has been said that it is impossible for anyone today to understand the *David*, situated as it is in the Academy, where everything about it appears grotesquely out of proportion.

*National Museum (Bargello)
Donatello, Marzocco.
The lion with
the fleur-de-lys,
symbol of the
Republic of Florence .*

A good eye and an evil tongue

The *Hercules and Cacus* by Bandinelli was supposed to symbolise victory over internal enemies, just as *David* represented victory over external enemies; it was placed here in 1534, and from the very beginning was insulted and mocked. Cellini welcomed it with many insulting comments, such as "an old sack full of melons". Perhaps the work is really less ugly than most people thought, but it is a clear example of what forced and unnatural results the idea of "novelty at all costs" can lead to in artistic endeavour. We must remember that Bandinelli, obstinate and presumptuous, had initially regarded the brutal figures as "too sweet", and retouched them to make them "cruder".

After the triumph of Michelangelo and the failure of Bandinelli, sculpting for the square had become an ambitious and risky task. Cellini when he returned to Florence in 1545, by this time internationally famous as a goldsmith, wanted to show his abilities as a sculptor. He begged Cosimo to allow him to try to make "a large statue, in marble and bronze", although realizing that "in the square there are statues by the great Donatello and the marvellous Michelangelo, who are two of the greatest men since classical times." In 1554 Cellini's *Perseus* was finished and placed in the loggia: if we look at it we can see that it has tried to combine the heroic strength of the *David*, and the tense vitality of the *Judith*. Although large and heavy as a whole, it is elegantly finished in all its details, especially the delicately ornate base, rather mannerist in its elegance; the beautiful and satanic head of the Medusa, a real "fleur du mal", is the utmost in stylistic achievement. The *Perseus* exemplifies the dualism of Cellini's aspirations, the "sweet" and the "terrible" which only Michelangelo had managed to combine. A hostile contemporary, Alfonso dei Pazzi, also felt some kind of dualism in this statue, and he wrote: "The body of an old man and the legs of a girl, this is what the new Perseus has, and all in all it may seem beautiful but is not worth anything." Even Bandinelli tried to get his own back, by comparing the work to an executioner showing the head of the executed; but apart from these isolated instances, Cellini received the praise he deserved.

Giambologna's *Rape of the Sabine Women* received only praise, but it is a work of a more controlled stylistic excellence. The *Perseus*, like the *David*, can be looked at from many angles, each revealing a different aspect of the whole, whereas Giambologna's work has been considered the first group of figures in European sculpture to be conceived without a main viewpoint: that means that the proportions and perspectives are perfect no matter which side one looks from. Giambologna also wanted to portray three different types of the human body: the old body of the conquered man, the full virility of the abductor, and the delicate feminine body of the woman in his arms. He also wanted to sculpt a figure higher off the ground than had ever been done before, and to create a group of three figures, not two like the *Judith and Holophernes*, and the *Hercules and Cacus*, . The subject matter of the composition did not really interest him at all. It was only after the statue had been finished and placed in the loggia that a scholar, Borghini, gave it the title of *Rape of Sabine Women*: then Giambologna added the bas-relief on the base, which explains the title.

This masterpiece by Giambologna brings us almost to the Baroque, and it is one of the obvious inspirations for some of Bernini's work (for example, the *Rape of Proserpina* in the Borghese Gallery in Rome). But in Bernini the figures are moving in space, (for example, *Apollo and Daphne* also in the Borghese Gallery), the marble is made to imitate the texture of skin, and the whole becomes as narrative as poetry; in Giambologna, still very much an artist of the sixteenth century, the figures turn in space but are closed in their own perfection, the material gives a sense of likeness, but does not imitate realistically, and the art is more concerned with form than content.

Also by Giambologna in the loggia is the *Hercules with the Centaur* (1559), placed here in 1842, originally on a street corner between the

Loggia dei Lanzi
Late Roman art,
Female figure.

▶

Giuseppe Zocchi,
the Uffizi Gallery
seen from the river
(eighteenth-century
engraving).

Cathedral and the church of Santa Maria Novella. The loggia also houses six Roman statues of matrons, a Greek sculpture of *Menelaus holding Patroclus' body*, and the *Rape of Polyxena*, by Fedi, sculpted in 1866. This is a fairly good piece and was praised: but the Florentines enjoyed pointing out that here the Greek hero is naked but for his helmet, whereas in a statue of General Fanti in the square of San Marco, Fedi protrayed him completely covered in a cloak but hatless. There were many other satiric things written about this statue. Already in 1577, Vincenzo Borghini had warned the architect Buontalenti that in Florence he should be careful, "because this city has a good eye but an evil tongue . . ."

The Uffizi

The square in front of the Uffizi, together with most of the rest of the city centre, has been closed to traffic; under the arcades there is a market of stalls selling souvenirs for tourists. But once upon a time it was not like this, and it was often compared to St. Mark's Square in Venice, although much narrower. It is possible that Vasari, the architect of this courtyard, which is also a street and a square, was inspired by the square Sansovino had recently designed in Venice. It stands at right angles to the larger square, as does the one in Venice, and, although it does not open out on to the lagoon, it overlooks, rather more modestly, the Arno.

Apart from a few chronological problems raised by modern critics, such as whether the first floor of the Uffizi was initially planned as a loggia, as it is now, or whether this was added after Vasari's death, we can say that the building was from the beginning intended to be impressive. Cosimo I had it built in order to house all the offices of the city's complex bureaucracy in one building. Vasari wrote of its architecture: "Never before have I designed anything so difficult or dangerous to build, because its foundations are in the river, and it almost stands on air." The building is characterized by the alternation of full and empty spaces, of "pietra serena", the famous Tuscan stone, and of white plaster, giving rise to the typically Florentine Renaissance contrast, interrupted rhythmically by niches, columns, portals, windows, and loggias. The construction took twenty years, from 1560 to 1580.

In 1581, however, the building was given a new function, which was to make its name famous throughout the world, beyond the merits of its architecture: Francesco I, who had succeeded Cosimo, began to use the upper loggia as a museum. The ceilings of the first floor corridors were decorated with elegant grotesques; classical statues and busts, portraits of famous men and self-portraits of artists were placed along the walls. Later the rooms off the corridor were also turned into a museum. In 1584 Buontalenti built the lavish *Tribuna*, which was to have been the centre of the gallery, where all the most precious objects were to be placed (jewels, bronzes, medals, the paintings of Raphael and of Andrea del Sarto, etc.) This room also had a complex cosmological meaning: here is the symbolisation of Air, in the windcock connected to the outside; of Water, in the dome studded with mother of pearl; of Fire, in the brilliant red tapestries on all the walls; and of Earth, the floor being mainly green in colour. There are also allusions to the Medici and to the figure of the Prince. In the first section of the building (the part closest to Palazzo Vecchio), the Medici Theatre was built in 1586, where spectacular performances took place. There was also a hanging garden with a fountain by Giambologna and a greenhouse was built on the terrace above the Loggia dei Lanzi. In the afternoons the grand dukes would sit on this terrace to listen to the music being played by the band in the Piazza Signoria. During the reign of Ferdinand, the upper floor of the western side of the Uffizi was used as a workshop by artisans; such as semi-precious stone workers, miniaturists, and watchmakers. There was also a "Fonderia" that is a pharmacy where perfumes, poisons and medicines were mixed. In 1600 Pigafetta wrote, describing this strange building in Florence which was half administrative and political offices and half artistic workshops: "The Uffizi . . . a new building of elegant architecture . . . where underneath are the offices of the city and courtcases are heard and the notaries keep their office. Above . . . is the Gallery, so-called in the French way, where there are innumerable wonderful things . . ."

Thus the Gallery was built and, unlike most museums which were not opened to the public until the late eighteenth century, it could be visited by anyone on request. The Uffizi will soon celebrate its four hundredth anniversary, but the history of the collection is too vast a subject to summarize here: the reader may refer to a book on this subject by the same author and the same publisher. It is enough here to give a few figures and data: in paintings alone the Uffizi possesses approximately 2500 items; in

1972 the Gallery was visited by more than a million people. The Gallery on the top floor is no longer large enough, even with the recent addition of the Vasari Corridor, for an orderly exhibition of the works of art, or to accommodate the ever-increasing number of visitors. It is now officially known that there is a project to extend the Gallery to include the entire building transferring the State Archives, placed here in 1852, elsewhere. This project, commonly referred to as "the greater Uffizi", is not due simply to megalomania, but to objective necessity. After the developments and additions of four centuries, it is necessary to increase the space, in an attempt to maintain the atmosphere and structure of the Gallery as it was seen by Pigafetta in 1600.

The Vasari Corridor

We have mentioned the unique Vasari Corridor, which was built on an idea of Cosimo I, and constructed with extraordinary speed between March and November 1565, in order to be completed before the wedding of Francesco to Joan of Austria in December. Francesco, who had already been made Prince Regent, was to live with his wife in Palazzo Vecchio, while Cosimo lived on the other side of the Arno in Palazzo Pitti. Perhaps some learned friend told Cosimo that Homer describes a passageway connecting Piram's palace with Hector's, and Cosimo probably decided that it would be a good idea to join the two palaces to provide an escape route in case of danger, and also to facilitate communications between the two without having to go into the streets of the city. But how to do it? The Uffizi which had already been started and which reached to the Arno, gave Vasari the idea.

Vasari first joined the Palazzo Vecchio to the Uffizi with a high bridge; then along the river he separated the Corridor from the Gallery, it joins the Ponte Vecchio after a stretch of arcades. It passes along the bridge above the shops and houses, and after another bridge, spanning a street, it carries on past the church of Santa Felicita and reaches the Boboli Gardens and the Pitti itself. From the windows there are wonderful views of the streets; by the church of Santa Felicita there is a large window, looking into the church, where the grand dukes could attend mass unseen. At a certain point in the corridor there were also steps leading down to a 'bathroom'. Later, carriages for two people, hand-pulled, were installed to make the journey even more comfortable. The corridor was used during the last war to connect the two parts of the city divided by the river; all the bridges had been destroyed except the Ponte Vecchio, but it was unusable because obstructed by rubble. The headquarters of the Allies could thus be kept informed by the partisans fighting in the centre of the city, which was still occupied by the Germans. After long years of restoration the corridor is now open to the public. In it are exhibited about 700 paintings, for which there is no longer room in the main gallery: these include a collection of seventeenth and eighteenth-century paintings, the collection of Italian and foreign self-portraits, and part of the iconographical collection. Thus, in theory, a visitor entering Palazzo Vecchio, can see kilometers and kilometers of museums: Palazzo Vecchio, the Uffizi, the Vasari Corridor, Palazzo Pitti, and even, through the Boboli Gardens, the Belvedere Fortress, on the outskirts of the city, travelling in a magical city within the city, which was once reserved to the grand dukes and their court.

Interior of the church of Santa Felicita seen from the Vasari Corridor.
The Grand Dukes could attend mass from here.

*"Lo scoppio del carro"
is a traditionally Florentine
way of celebrating Easter
Sunday.*

*On St. John the Baptist's
day there are always
elaborate fireworks displays.*

*"Il Calcio in costume" is a
game of football, played in
Renaissance costumes,
between the teams of the
four quarters of the city: San
Giovanni, Santa Croce,
Santa Maria Novella and
Santo Spirito.*

The Business Centre and Orsanmichele

The vast Piazza della Signoria served for political functions, for celebrations such as the feast day of St. John, the patron saint of Florence, when the representatives of all the towns under Florence's domination organized a procession to prove their loyalty to the city: or as a market for farmers (as is still the case every Friday around the equestrian statue of Cosimo). But is was in the nearby streets, especially in the area to the north-west, that the business centre of Florence really was.

In 1547 Cosimo I had Tasso build the loggia of the New Market, which had always been the meeting place for bankers and merchants. It was such an animated centre that a road nearby was re-christened 'Via del Baccano', literally 'the street of noise'. Today the New Market houses a very picturesque little market of straw goods. The larger Old Market was for foodstuffs, a real paradise for gluttons with its vast quantities of meat, fruits and vegetables: it was in a zone surrounded by taverns and inns of all kinds, and, on a column, stood a statue of *Abundance* by Donatello. Cosimo I also transferred the fish market here from the Ponte Vecchio. In 1560, under pressure from the Counter-Reformation, Cosimo created, to the north of the Old Market, the ghetto for the Jews. In the nineteenth century this zone was still populated by old monuments and buildings, but must have been very squalid and unhealthy. The zone was completely cleared up, and the present Piazza della Repubblica was created in 1890. The equestrian statue of King Victor Emmanuel, now in the park of the Cascine, was originally placed here. Although the square is not architecturally distinguished and the rebuilding might have been managed better, it did provide a solution to a problem which today, out of respect for the historical past, it would have been more difficult to solve.

But the building which really represented the Florence of the bankers, of the industrialists, of the merchants, the artisans and the professionals, was Orsanmichele, also originally a market place. Later the building was handed over to a consortium organised by the guild, which undertook its decoration. This palace had been built in the 1330s with the ground floor opening on to the streets through arcades, which were eventually closed off around 1380. Orsanmichele was dedicated to the worship of a supposedly miraculous image of the Madonna, for which Orcagna built the sumptuous tabernacle in 1359; the upper floors, however, were still used as a storing place for wheat and other cereals. Each guild had a tabernacle on the outside of the building, which housed a statue of its own patron saint. These statues were mostly sculpted and placed in their niches during the first decades of the fifteenth century, and many of them are achievements of considerable merit. There are for example, works by Nanni di Banco of a classical austerity; and Ghiberti's refined and elegant bronze of *St. Matthew* (1422), set in a Renaissance tabernacle; Donatello's *St. Mark* (1413), his gilt *St. Louis* (1423) later moved to Santa Croce, and above all his *St. George* (1416), the patron saint of Armourers, in warrior's dress. (The original is now in the Bargello.) This youthful warrior, so full of life and so proud, is the first embodiment of the new man of the Renaissance. The bas relief beneath the statue depicts *Saint George Killing the Dragon*, a miniature scene sculpted with such delicacy that we are given a perfect impression of receding layers of depth as far as the hills in the background, and of the trees swaying in the wind, through Donatello's consummate mastery of the science of perspective.

In the second half of the fifteenth century new sculptures were substituted in some niches, Verrocchio's *Doubting Thomas*, for example (1483), while Giambologna's *Saint Luke* was only put in place in 1601. Orsanmichele became, like the square in front of the Cathedral and the Piazza della Signoria, another museum in the midst of the city. And there can be no doubt that the taste of the Florentines, before there were museums, and even since then, was formed by the everyday experience of these masterpieces, placed here for everyone to see, without an entrance ticket or opening hours.

▶
General view of the centre of the city with Piazza della Signoria and the Palazzo Vecchio: the true civic centre of Florence.

Budapest, Szépmüveszéti Muzeum Bernardo Bellotto, Piazza della Signoria. The square has not changed much since this was painted in the eighteenth century: the church of San Romolo, which we can see on the left, has disappeared.

The palace of the Guild of Woolworkers.

◄
*Palazzo Vecchio
Courtyard.
Andrea del Verrocchio's
elegant fountain, the putto
with a dolphin, stands in the
centre of the first courtyard.
The stucco work on the
columns is a late sixteenth-
century addition.*

►
*Cortile della Dogana
(Customs Courtyard).
Solid fifteenth-century
construction below the
Salone dei Cinquecento
(Hall of the Five Hundred).*

*The arches of the gallery
which runs along the
battlements.*

*Fourteenth-century wooden
ceiling.
The gold fleurs-de-lys
represent the House of
Anjou, who protected the
Republic of Florence in the
thirteenth and fourteenth
centuries.*

*Eleonor of Toledo's
Apartments,
the Green Room.*

*Fourteenth-century
stairway leading to
the tower.*

*Palazzo Vecchio
Leo X's Apartments
Room of Cosimo the Elder.
Giorgio Vasari,
Cosimo returns from exile.
This painting is one of the
series depicting the life of
the founder of Medici
power.*

*Uffizi Gallery
Copy from
Leonardo da Vinci,
The Battle of Anghiari.
One of the copies of
Leonardo's famous fresco,
painted in 1502 in the Salone
dei Cinquecento, but later
destroyed.*

*"Salotta"
Fourteenth-century unknown
artist, St. Anne and the
Expulsion of
the Duke of Athens.
This happened in 1343 on
St. Anne's day.*

*Salone dei Cinquecento
Michelangelo, Victory.
Probably originally carved as
part of the tomb of Julius
II.*

▶

*Sala dei Gigli.
This large fifteenth-century
room was decorated by
Domenico Ghirlandaio with
portraits of famous Romans
and of saints. The lions
carry flags bearing the Cross
of the People and the fleur-
de-lys (giglio) of the
Commune.*

*Salone dei Cinquecento.
Built by Cronaca
(1495). On the walls are
frescoes by Giorgio. Vasari of
episodes from Florentine
history.*

*Cappella dei Priori.
Decorated by
Ridolfo del Ghirlandaio.
On the altar, Holy Family
by Mariano di Pescia.*

Studiolo of Francesco I.

◀
Museum of San Marco
Piazza della Signoria.
with the burning at the stake
of Savonarola and his
followers (1498).

Piazza della Signoria
Bartolomeo Ammannati,
Fountain of Neptune.
Popularly called "il
Biancone", the big white
one, this fountain, with its
bronze Tritons and Nereids,
is a good example of late
Florentine Mannerism
(1563-75).

▶

Donatello,
Judith and Holophernes.
Bronze statue, typical of the
artist's late period. It was
placed here when the Medici
were exiled in 1495.

Bartolomeo Ammannati,
Fonntain of Neptune.
Detail of one of the
horses of Neptune's
Chariot and of one
of the bronze Nereids.

View of Ammannati's statue
from the Loggia dei Lanzi.

View of all the
statues in the
square, looking
towards the Loggia
.dei Lanzi.

◄

*Loggia dei Lanzi
Typical Florentine Gothic
construction.*

*Loggia dei Lanzi.
Benvenuto Çellini, Perseus.
One of the few large works
by this Florentine artist
(1545-54).*

*Giambologna,
Rape of the Sabine
Women.
Fine example of the art of
the sculptor from Douai.
(1583).*

*Hellenistic art,
Menelaus holding
Patroclus' body.*

►

*Uffizi Gallery
One of the corridors on the
top floor of the building
built by Vasari to house the
offices of the Grand Duchy
(1560-80).*

*The 'Tribune'.
This room was built by
Bernardo Buontalenti
and housed the most
important works of art of
the Medici collection.*

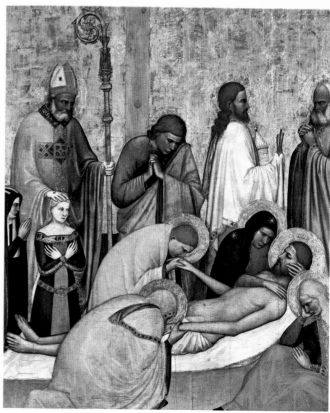

◄
Uffizi Gallery
Cimabue,
Madonna and Child.
Originally in the church of
Santa Trinita,
this is one of Cimabue's
masterpieces.

Giottino,
Lamentation (detail).
The work of one of Giotto's
most talented pupils, this
panel shows a definite
northern influence.

Pietro Lorenzetti,
Altarpiece of
the Blessed Umiltà detail .
This panel shows Giotto's
influence on this Sienese
painter of the early
fourteenth century.

Duccio di Buoninsegna,
Madonna and Child.
Originally in Santa Maria
Novella,
in the Rucellai Chapel.

▶
Giotto,
Ognissanti Madonna.
Painted around 1310 for the
high altar of the Franciscan
church.

Uffizi Gallery
Simone Martini,
Annunciation.
Painted in 1333 for the
Cathedral of Siena with the
help of his brother-in-law
Lippo Memmi.

Gentile da Fabriano,
Adoration of the Magi.
Painted in 1423 for the
church of Santa Trinita, it is
one of the most interesting
examples of International
Gothic in Florence.

▶
Paolo Uccello,
Battle of San Romano.
(detail).
The same event is depicted
in two other paintings by the
same artist; they are now in
London and Paris.

Piero della Francesca,
Portraits of
Federico di Montefeltro,
Lord of Urbino, and his
wife, Battista Sforza (1465).

Uffizi Gallery
Sandro Botticelli,
Primavera
(Allegory of Spring).
The composition, fully
Humanist in conception, was
painted in 1477-78 for
Lorenzo di Pierfrancesco
dei Medici.

Sandro Botticelli,
The Birth of Venus.
Painted around 1486 for
Lorenzo di Pierfrancesco
dei Medici.

▶

Hugo van der Goes,
Portinari Triptych.
Painted for the Medici agent
in Bruges,
Tommaso Portinari,
this work greatly influenced
Florentine painters of the
late fifteenth century.

Filippo Lippi,
Madonna and Child
with Angels.

◀
Uffizi Gallery
Leonardo da Vinci,
Adoration of the Magi.
One of the first Florentine
works of Leonardo's, it was
commissioned by the
monks
of San Donato Scopeto.
It was left unfinished when
Leonardo moved to Milan in
1482.

Leonardo da Vinci,
Annunciation.
Although no source
mentions this painting, it is
commonly attributed to
Leonardo and dated around
1472-75.

▶
Correggio,
Adoration, detail.

Michelangelo, Holy Family
(Tondo Doni).
Painted in 1504-5, it was the
starting point for the new
Mannerist trend.

▶▶
Following pages:
Raphael,
Madonna of the Goldfinch.
Painted in Florence for
Lorenzo Nasi in 1506.

Titian, Venus of Urbino.

Tintoretto, Leda and the
Swan.

◄
Parmigianino,
Madonna 'of the long neck',
detail.

Pontormo,
Supper at Emmaus.

Rembrandt,
Self-portrait, detail.

Rubens,
Triumphal entry of Henry IV
into Paris (detail).

►
Rosso Fiorentino,
Cherub playing a Lute.

Caravaggio,
Medusa.

◄

*Uffizi Gallery
The Vasari Corridor.
Built to join
Palazzo Vecchio to the
new Medici court
at Palazzo Pitti,
it contains the collection
of self-portraits
and iconographical
collection.*

*The Vasari Corridor
crosses the river
Arno along the
Ponte Vecchio.*

►

*Orsanmichele
One of the most
characteristic
of Florentine buildings,
this church-cum-granary
was decorated by great
artists commissioned
by the Guilds.*

*Andrea del Verrocchio,
Doubting Thomas.*

*Andrea Orcagna,
Marble Tabernacle
(detail).
Carved between 1349 and
1359 it is a great example of
Florentine Gothic sculpture.
This detail shows the
Assumptiom of the Virgin.*

*Luca della Robbia,
Madonna and Child.
Coat-of-arms of the Guild of
Doctors and Apothecaries.*

(illustrations
from page 113 to page 126)

The Medici in their Palace

◄

*Laurentian Library,
'Biadaiolo' manuscript.
Distribution of wheat in
Orsanmichele.*

When the Medici family became the masters of the city, the part of Florence in which they lived to the north of the Cathedral became very important. The family had previously owned towers and houses near the old market, and a little street near the present Piazza della Repubblica is still called Via dei Medici. But in the second half of the fourteenth century the family moved to the neighbourhood of San Lorenzo. Giovanni di Bicci dei Medici, in the early fifteenth century, lived first in Via Larga (now Via Cavour) and later in the Cathedral Square, where he must have witnessed the building of Brunelleschi's dome. This Medici, who has since been overshadowed by the fame of his successors, was of solid peasant stock and rough in appearance, but was also an extremely able financier who accumulated a vast fortune and in a cautious and far-seeing manner unusual for his times, drew support from the people; Manetti, a contemporary of his, claims that he was also a man of great artistic taste. In 1401 he was one of the judges of the famous competition for the doors of the Baptistry, which was won by Ghiberti; it seems that later he also financed the monument to the anti-Pope John XXIII (his friend Baldassarre Coscia) in the Baptistry, built by Donatello and Michelozzo around 1427. He is also supposed to have contributed financially to the Hospital of the Innocents and he was certainly an admirer of Brunelleschi's revolutionary architecture. Thus, when the reconstruction of San Lorenzo was begun in brick, and Brunelleschi (from whom Giovanni had commissioned a chapel and the sacristy) proposed a different plan for the church on a more ambitious scale, Giovanni did not hesitate to commit himself to financing the entire enterprise. And so the Basilica of San Lorenzo, the first to be built in Renaissance style, was begun in 1421.

Work started on the Old Sacristy which, with its complex geometrical structure, created such amazement among the Florentines that there was a continuous stream of visitors often interrupting the work. Giovanni di Bicci died in 1429 and was buried in the centre of that sacristy in a sarcophagus also Renaissance in style. San Lorenzo was to be the burial place of all the Medici after him for over three centuries, in more and more elaborate tombs and buried with funerals of great splendour.

*Codice Rustici
Fifteenth-century Ms.,
San Marco.*

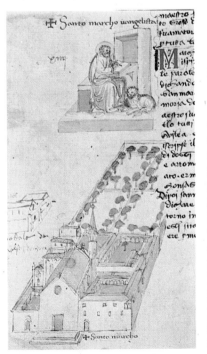

Cosimo the Elder and San Marco

Cosimo, Giovanni's son, had a true passion for building. Brunelleschi had convinced him that buildings last for hundreds and thousands of years and continue to bring glory to whoever had them built. Vasari says that Cosimo continued to commission buildings until he died, and all the time the work on San Lorenzo progressed. But Brunelleschi's plans, conceived on a grand scale, took too long to build for a man whose practical sense made him anxious to see the finished product. His favourite architect was in fact Michelozzo, who had followed him into temporary exile in Venice in 1433, where he had already started working for him. Michelozzo was given the task of the complete reconstruction of the monastery of San Marco, where Cosimo, not far from his own house, installed a group of reformed Dominicans whose protector and financial supporter he became. Within a few years Michelozzo had finished the project which was immediately praised for its practical layout and design, with two large cloisters and two small ones, vegetable gardens and orchards at the back (personally supervised by Cosimo), two refectories, a hospice, a chapter hall and a church, and on the first floor vast dormitories divided into cells and a library. This library was richly stocked and, the first in the world to be open to all scholars. The total expence incurred in this project was calculated at 40,000 florins. What strikes today's visitor is the combination of extreme sobriety and sophistication of the monastery. (It seems that the Dominicans curbed Cosimo's desire for grandeur.) The walls are covered with pale plaster both in the cloisters and in the library: the arches span lightly over the Ionic columns where the effect is of a space created by pure lines and light, spiritual and abstract like the purpose of San Marco itself. In harmony with Michelozzo's architecture are the equally pure, simple yet deeply moving paintings by Beato Angelico, who, while a friar in the monastery, decorated it with frescoes.

The rector of San Marco was Antonino Pierozzi, later the Archbishop of Florence and then canonized. He kept a cell permanently reserved for Cosimo, where he might retire for his private meditations. Cosimo could not have imagined that there would come a time when this religious institution would turn hostile towards his successors. In 1481 the Ferrarese monk Girolamo Savonarola came to San Marco, and his bitter sermons helped to bring about the fall and the exile of Cosimo's great-grandson Piero dei Medici in 1494. But, as Cosimo liked to say, "states cannot be ruled by prayers", and in 1498 Savonarola was forced to give himself up to his enemies after a night of resistance in the monastery. Savonarola had ordered the burning of many books and paintings which he considered pagan and profane, and now a fire was waiting for the defeated prophet-preacher in the Piazza della Signoria.

Medici-Riccardi Palace.

The building of the palace

Before building a new palace, which was to be something between a private house and the palace of a ruler, both a family residence and the central office for all political and economic matters, Cosimo waited ten years after his return from exile, until such time as he felt secure against any political upheaval in Florence. Brunelleschi presented him with a plan which seems to have been for a palace just opposite San Lorenzo, isolated from other houses; but Cosimo rejected it because he thought it "too great and sumptuous an undertaking", wary of causing envy among those Florentine magnates who, until recently, had been his equals. Cosimo always regarded envy as a danger to be avoided: he used to say that envy was a dangerous weed which must be allowed to dry up and not be watered. Eventually Michelozzo was given the task, and the palace he built on Via Larga combines elements both from Brunelleschi and Leon Battista Alberti. Functional and comfortable inside, the facade and courtyard of this palace are divided into three distinct and graded levels, typical of the architecture of the time: the ground floor is powerful and heavy with its blocks of rusticated stone and its porticoed courtyard, while the first floor is lighter with its gracefully mullioned windows; the second floor, with smooth facings which opened out on to a loggia, is infinitely more delicate. This palace served as a model for all those that were built by the Florentine magnates of the century: Cosimo had not crushed them, but encouraged them to emulate him. Although begun as early as 1444, Cosimo was not able to live in his palace until 1459, only five years before his death. Having lost his second-born, Giovanni, and with his eldest son Piero the Gouty in poor health, Cosimo did not feel comfortable in such a large building: "too big a house for so small a family", he used to say. But perhaps, even behind his lament, was the cleverness of the old fox taking care not to nourish envy.

There is no room here to list all of Cosimo's building enterprises in

*San Marco
Fra' Bartolommeo,
Portrait of
Girolamo Savonarola.*

Florence and villas in the countryside around the city, all built by Michelozzo. He even commissioned buildings in Jerusalem and Paris. This passion for building was closely linked with a more general passion for culture, which has been exaggerated perhaps by his admirers and underestimated by others, such as Machiavelli who referred to him as "a man without culture". His contemporaries called him "the great merchant", the man who for thirty years held Florence in his hand by means of a series of astute political moves, the protector of artists such as Donatello, and of scholars, and a collector of ancient manuscripts. He died in 1464: and although he had left instructions for a simple funeral, he was, quite understandably, buried with great pomp. He was proclaimed "Pater Patriae" (Father of his Country) and was buried in the transept in San Lorenzo, inside a column symbolizing his strength and importance.

Medici-Riccardi Palace
The courtyard.

Piero the Gouty

Coat-of arms and seal of Piero the Gouty.

Of Cosimo's four sons the beautiful Giovanni had been a pleasure-loving young man, not at all keen to "mind the shop", as was still, somewhat severely, expected of Medici sons. Women, food and drink undermined his health, although he was basically a strong man, and he died before his father. Florence, however, had been fond of this gay character who loved the arts, books, music and poetry. By a Circassian slave, Cosimo had also had an illegitimate son, Carlo who was given the post of Rector of the Cathedral of Prato, where he supervised the completion of the famous frescoes in the choir by Filippo Lippi.

Piero, the eldest son, passed into history with the unglorious nickname of "the Gouty", after the illness from which he suffered; and, placed as he was between his father Cosimo and his son Lorenzo the Magnificent, he has never enjoyed great fame. And yet culturally he is an extremely interesting figure, representing a much more sophisticated taste and an outlook not confined to his Florentine environment. In 1438 Domenico Veneziano asked to come to Florence to work for him, promising him "marvellous things" and wanting to compete with Lippi and Fra Angelico. Roger van der Weyden, the great Flemish master who came to Italy for the Jubilee in 1459, painted two paintings for the Medici possibly on Piero's commission: the *Deposition* in the Uffizi Gallery and the *Madonna with Saints* now in Frankfurt. Andrea del Castagno portrayed Piero wearing a Burgundian turban in a portrait now in Zurich; Piero also sent agents to buy tapestries for him in Flanders. When Gozzoli, in 1460, decorated the chapel of Palazzo Medici in a very splendid and magnificent style recalling the tradition of Gentile da Fabriano, we know from certain documents that not only did Piero commission the work, but he followed its progress very carefully. In the *Procession of the Magi*, against a Tuscan landscape background are portrayed the chief characters who attended the famous Ecumenical Council held in Florence in 1439, all in contemporary dress, and other celebrities present at the festivities held in honour of Pope Pius II's visit to the city in 1459. Piero appears on the right-hand wall wearing a red hat and riding a white horse, preceded by his groom with his emblem, a diamond point inscribed with the word "Semper". But, perhaps with prophetic intuition, the painter placed in front of him his young son Lorenzo. On the end wall we can see Piero's three daughters Maria, Bianca and Nannina, portrayed on horseback. The floor is decorated with inlaid marble.

The entire decoration of the palace was followed very closely by Piero, who was kept away from the affairs of state by his illness: patronising the arts and increasing his collections seem to have given him some respite from ill health. His young son Lorenzo's room was decorated in 1456-7 with Paolo Uccello's three Battles (now in Florence, London and Paris), with a battle between dragons and lions and a scene from the legend of Paris also by Uccello, and a hunting scene by Pesellino. Piero's little study was filled with glazed terracottas by Luca della Robbia, among them the *Months* which are now in the Victoria and Albert Museum in London. In 1460 Pollaiolo painted three large canvasses of the *Labours of Hercules* for one of the halls of the palace. There was also a *St. John* by Andrea del Castagno, and Donatello's *Judith*, now in Piazza della Signoria, was placed in the courtyard as a fountain. Piero's other contributions to the city's art heritage also show his taste for an elaborate sophistication: Fra Angelico, on his commission, painted the wooden doors of a cupboard for the silver of the church of Santissima Annunziata (now in the Museum of San Marco); and Michelozzo was commissioned to build, at San Miniato al Monte, a tabernacle "of great appearance and expense", decorated with terracottas by Luca della Robbia.

Despite his illness, Piero had been able to deal with a serious conspiracy in 1466 and its various after effects; by 1469, although almost completely paralyzed by gout, one can say that he was even more powerful than Cosimo had been. In February of that year a splendid joust took place in Piazza

Santa Croce, in honour of the forthcoming wedding of his son Lorenzo to Clarice Orsini of Rome. This was the first time that a wife had been chosen for a member of the Medici from outside Florence; Piero himself had married Lucrezia Tornabuoni, a Florentine. The joust was won by Lorenzo, although he admitted himself that perhaps his victory was not entirely due to his skill. The wedding took place in June and a banquet which lasted three days was held in the garden and the loggias of the palace in Via Larga. Magnificent presents were sent from everywhere including 150 calves, more than 4000 chickens and capons, and vast quantities of Tuscan and foreign wine. But on December 2nd, sooner than had been expected, Piero died; he suffered from aphasia and could not speak; he died without making a confession or a will. A witness writes that 'he watched all who came and said nothing'.

"Pleasure at the Helm"

Two days after Piero's death, a delegation of citizens came to Lorenzo to ask him to take over the position of leadership already held by his father and grandfather. Lorenzo accepted, calculating that without holding power in the city it would be difficult for him to keep his wealth. With the power in Palazzo Medici in the hands of two young men, Lorenzo and his younger brother Giuliano, Florence appeared to be, in the words of a contemporary, a city "with youth at the prow and pleasure at the helm".

In 1471 Galeazzo Maria Sforza, Duke of Milan, and his wife Bona of Savoy, visited Florence escorted by a spectacular entourage; they stayed at the Medici Palace and Sforza declared that nowhere in Italy had he seen such a wondrous collection of works of art. In 1475 a second exceptional joust was held in Piazza Santa Croce, this time in honour of Giuliano and his mistress, the young Simonetta Cattaneo, Vespucci by marriage. Poliziano wrote a poem about this tournament and it inspired, perhaps indirectly, Botticelli's masterpieces, the *Primavera* and the *Birth of Venus* at the Uffizi and the *Venus and Mars* in London. In this last painting it is traditional to identify the two figures as Giuliano and Simonetta. The three generations of the Medici also appear in Botticelli's *Adoration of the Magi*, painted probably around 1475: Cosimo the Elder, his son Piero and his grandsons Lorenzo and Giuliano, the present rulers. Simonetta died the following year of consumption, and Giuliano, who was expected to become a cardinal, was murdered in the Cathedral in 1478, in the abortive Pazzi conspiracy. Lorenzo survived this and the wars which followed, and eventually became a major figure in Italian politics. In his palace two future popes were growing up: Giuliano's illegitimate son Giulio, who was to become Clement VII, and Lorenzo's own son Giovanni, who became pope before Clement VII, as Leo X. Lorenzo's eldest son Piero, like his father, married an Orsini; and one of his daughters, Maddalena, married Franceschetto Cibo, son of Pope Innocent VIII. By this time Savonarola, preaching from the monastery of San Marco, was beginning to predict divine punishment but Lorenzo took no steps to prevent his preaching. On being elected prior of the monastery built by the Medici, Savonarola had not even been, to pay homage to Lorenzo, as was the custom. Though the city was generally prosperous the Medici's own finances were not flourishing: Lorenzo was not an astute merchant and many times had to accept loans. But he was not over worried by the situation: in his *Ricordi* (Memories) he writes that "a great sum has been spent by our family from the year 1434 until now (1471), as is shown in a notebook . . . an incredible sum which is more than 663,755 florins, on alms, buildings and taxes, not counting other expenses; but I do not wish to have and regrets, for, although some people might have preferred to have money in their purses, I judge this amount to have been well spent in giving honour to our state". His strength lay in his optimism and in his liberality; his motto in his youth, had been "Le temps revient", and he had written famous lines on the beauty of youth with the advice "Let who would be, now be merry; Sure is no one of tomorrow". He loved both the sophistication of city life and the relaxation of the country, both the life of the senses and the life of the intellect. His enemies say that he had a corrupting influence on his fellow citizens, but, in the final analysis, the years of his rule were the most splendid and the most memorable years in the history of the city.

Lorenzo the Magnificent and the Arts

What Lorenzo the Magnificent represents as a man of culture is well-known: he was a good poet and a neo-Platonist philosopher, a follower of Ficino, Alberti, Landino, Poliziano and Pico della Mirandola. Subtle allegorical interpretations, references to the philosophy and the myths of classical times, gave the Florentine circle a very special brand of intellectual distinction, never separated from the cult of formal beauty. It is enough to contrast Lorenzo's interpretation of love as "appetite for the beautiful" with the conception of love as sex, to understand the spirituality which for them was part of the reality of life. Physically ugly and with an unpleasant voice, Lorenzo was fascinating for his manner, his sense of measure and balance, and his sophistication. All the major artists of the second half of the fifteenth century were patronised by him. In 1472 Verrocchio built the tombs in San Lorenzo for Piero and Giovanni, Lorenzo's father and uncle; he also sculpted the young *David*, now in the Bargello, for Lorenzo and Giuliano, which was later given to the Signoria together with the *Putto with Dolphin*, also originally made for Lorenzo. The *Woman with a Bouquet*, in the Bargello, on which Leonardo probably also worked, is supposed to be a portrait of Lucrezia Donati, Lorenzo's platonic love: he wrote of her hands as the most beautiful ever created by nature, and in this bust the hands which inspired the poem are perhaps over emphasised, as though the commissioner had expressly asked for them to stand out.

In 1489 Lorenzo wrote about Antonio Pollaiolo: "He is the most important artist in this city". His bronze statue of *Hercules and Antaeus*, now in the Bargello, was originally in the Medici Palace. Botticelli painted his *Pallas and the Centaur* (now in the Uffizi) for Lorenzo; Signorelli painted for him a pagan *Feast of Pan* (destroyed), and his villa of Spedaletto, near Volterra, was frescoed around 1483 by Botticelli, Perugino, Ghirlandaio and Filippino Lippi. And in any case Lorenzo's patronage of the arts must not only be judged by works he commissioned for himself, but also by how he helped artists obtain other commissions, from public or private sources, in Florence and outside. In the field of architecture Lorenzo was a friend of Leon Battista Alberti's, whom he helped overcome the various difficulties in

Museo degli Argenti Francesco Furini, Lorenzo the Magnificent and the Platonic Academy in the Medici villa of Careggi.

finishing the tribune of Santissima Annunziata; but his principal architect was Giuliano da Sangallo, just as Michelozzo had been for Cosimo. Sangallo built the villa at Poggio a Caiano for him not far from Florence; but Lorenzo, unlike Cosimo, no longer had the wealth required for grandiose constructions and, although he would have liked to enlarge and beautify the city, he never could afford the expense. We must also mention the Medici garden of San Marco, the purpose of which was both to house statues and paintings and to serve as a school for artists under the guidance of the sculptor Bertoldo, who had the good fortune to have Michelangelo as a pupil.

When Lorenzo died in 1492 an inventory was made of Palazzo Medici which still exists: the collection of marbles, tapestries, cameos, jewels and precious objects of all kinds, is incredible. Among the paintings were Byzantine icons, works by Giotto, Masaccio, Fra Angelico, Van Eyck, Petrus Christus, Domenico Veneziano, Squarcione, etc. Among the sculptures were works by Donatello, Mino da Fiesole, Desiderio da Settignano and many others. The Medici Palace was already a museum and there was no foreigner who came to Florence who did not ask to see it.

From the Medici to the Riccardi to the State

The death of Lorenzo, killed by gout at the age of forty-three, is said to have been preceded by warning omens: two days before, a thunderbolt struck the dome of the Cathedral and cracked a marble rib on the side facing the Medici Palace; two lions tore each other to pieces in the menagerie behind the Palazzo Vecchio; a comet appeared above the villa at Careggi, where Lorenzo died; and the day after his death his personal doctor was found dead at the bottom of a well, by suicide or murder.

Lorenzo's successor, his young son Piero, possessed many negative qualities: lack of intelligence, presumption, haughtiness and impulsiveness. He used Michelangelo's genius to carve a statue out of snow, a masterpiece which melted away within a few days; at a ball once he slapped a cousin, thus adding a branch of his own family to the long list of his enemies. During the invasion of Italy by Charles VIII, in 1494, he committed a series of strategical and tactical errors, which culminated in the surrender of the fortresses of Sarzana and Pietrasanta to the French king. This caused anti-Medicean feeling in Florence to run high and Piero tried to reassert himself in the city by force; but his enemies forestalled him and on November 9th of that year Piero had to flee on horseback towards Bologna, having been declared a rebel and with a heavy price on his head. The Medici Palace, labelled as the house of the tyrants, was plundered by the angry population, but the government quickly confiscated what was left, some of which was transferred to Palazzo Vecchio, and the rest was auctioned at Orsanmichele. The greatest collection of fifteenth-century art, accumulated over many years, was thus dispersed. In the meantime, on November 14th, Charles VIII was received as a guest in the confiscated palace; this event is represented in a painting by Granacci.

The palace was returned to the Medici when they forced their way back into Florence in 1512; but when Giuliano, the first to return, entered the city, he found the palace so empty and ruined that he installed himself temporarily elsewhere. Piero had died in 1503 and now his brothers, one of whom was the cardinal Giovanni (later to become Pope Leo X), lived in the palace together with their nephew, Piero's son, Lorenzo di Piero and with their cousin Giulio, also a cardinal and a future pope (Clement VII). More work was done on the palace, including the shutting off of the loggia with windows designed by Michelangelo. They started having Medicean banquets and feasts again, organized by Lorenzo, who had become the Duke of Urbino, and Giuliano, the Duke of Nemours. When these two dukes died and when, in 1523, Giulio became pope, the palace was inhabited only by children in the care of Cardinal Passerini: Ippolito, the illegitimate son of the Duke of Nemours, Caterina, daughter of the Duke of Urbino and future Queen of France, and Alessandro, the illegitimate son supposedly of the Duke of Urbino, but in fact of Pope Clement VII.

Alessandro dei Medici.

The Sack of Rome in 1527 caused a revolt against the Medici in Florence and the cardinal was forced to flee with the two bastards in his charge. The Medici Palace was once again sacked and plundered, and the Medici crest was replaced by the Cross of the People. On July 5th 1531, after the siege and surrender of Florence, Alessandro was reinstated as Duke and leader of the city. Just as Machiavelli had predicted, the logic of politics implied that every time the Medici were reinstated, they must become more authoritarian, more severe and dictatorial in the exercise of power. Violent and licentious, the young Alessandro raped Florentine women, even the nuns in the convents, he humiliated the local aristocracy, and he terrorized the population with sentences of exile or death. He loved to affect a Florentine accent, but, for personal protection, was surrounded by paid foreign bodyguards. His major construction was the building, in 1534, of the Fortezza da Basso, the purpose of which was to prevent a Florentine rebellion, a more pressing danger than any foreign hostilities. The city, in particular the aristocracy, tried to rebel; many had left the city, including the very powerful Strozzi family, but Alessandro was supported both by the pope and the Emperor Charles V, whose daughter he married. Charles V stayed in the palace when he came to Florence in 1536, and was followed by the arrival of Alessandro's wife-to-be, an illegitimate daughter of the emperor's, Marguerite of Austria. On the night of January 6th 1537, Alessandro's cousin Lorenzino lured the Duke into his house with the promise of a night with the woman he desired, and succeeded in murdering him. This action recalled Brutus and Caesar, but Florence was incapable of rebellion. In fact, the house of the murderer was destroyed, and a few days later the eighteen-year old Cosimo dei Medici was proclaimed Alessandro's successor. The militia took the opportunity to plunder the Medici Palace. In 1539 Cosimo had taken his bride, Eleonor of Toledo, to the palace, but on May 15th 1540 he abandoned it forever and moved into the Palazzo Vecchio to assert his hold over the city even more firmly.

The palace then passed to minor branches of the family until in 1659 it was sold to the Marquis Gabriello Riccardi. The palace became a rich and aristocratic residence: the facade was enlarged, although the addition was built in Michelozzo's style, and the interior was transformed by grandiose Baroque decoration to its present appearance, including the sumptous frescoes by Luca Giordano. In 1780 the Riccardi family gave a splendid banquet for the Grand Duke Peter Leopold of Lorraine, with 4,000 guests; after this, the palace was opened to the public for two days and 30,000 people visited it without damaging anything. The Florentines had become respectful.

Finally, in 1814, after a lavish farewell banquet, the Riccardi handed over the Palace to the grand-ducal government. It was clumsily converted to house offices: first the city guards and other local authorities; then, when Florence became capital of Italy, the Ministry of the Interior, and now the offices of the province and the regional prefecture. Not until 1911 was any restoration begun, and in 1929 the ground floor was transformed into a museum where, ten years later, an exhibition took place dedicated to the most famous, the most loved and the most hated family of Florence, the Medici.

The three sacristies of San Lorenzo

The later history of the Medici will be narrated in chapters relating to Palazzo Vecchio and Palazzo Pitti; but, even after they had moved from a private residence to a court, their burial place was always San Lorenzo: their last journey was always to their local parish church. So it was for the funeral of Grand Duke Cosimo I, in 1574; the procession traversed almost the entire city and ended at San Lorenzo, the church was draped with black hangings, painted with skeletons and with scenes celebrating the first grand-duke, and in the transept stood the funeral catafalque surmounted by a pyramid of lighted candles.

The Medici tombs were also works of art of the highest order. The three different sacristies epitomize three different periods of art: the Old Sacristy built by Brunelleschi, the New Sacristy by Michelangelo, and the Chapel of the Princes. The Old Sacristy, with its purity of light, and the refined elegance of Verrocchio's fifteenth-century tomb, is neatly contrasted by Michelangelo's fully developed and dramatic classicism. This new sacristy was commissioned by Cardinal Giulio, later Pope Clement VII, who wanted a grand burial place for Giuliano and Lorenzo the Magnificent, for Giuliano Duke of Nemours, Lorenzo Duke of Urbino, Leo X and for himself. A continuous struggle took place between the Medici cardinal, who had his own ideas about the project, and the artist, jealously guarding his plans and always reasserting his artistic independence. For example, in 1526, Pope Clement said of the tombs which had been planned for Leo X and for himself: "He can do as he wishes in the rest of the sacristy, but for my tomb and Leo's he must do as I wish". Michelangelo was forced to interrupt his work during the period of the Medici exile from Florence, from 1527 to 1531; during this time he joined the ranks of the anti-Mediceans. Yet after their return he took up the work again, but as he wrote, "more out of fear than love". But in 1534 Pope Clement died and Michelangelo left Florence forever: the work, although not completed, was abandoned. Among the first visitors to the sacristy was Charles V. A contemporary observer wrote that "he went before leaving Florence (May 4th 1534) to hear a mass in the church of San Lorenzo, and after the mass he went to see the marvellous sacristy built in that church by Michelangelo Buonarroti, a Florentine sculptor, who can be deservedly called one of the lights of Florentine glory; then he mounted his horse". What can the impressions of the powerful but melancholy emperor have been? Thousands of pages of critical work have been written in an attempt to reveal the meaning of this rather small room. Yet, in it one can almost feel the silent power and the symbolic presence of superhuman powers, the mystery of the world, the feeling of "Time which wastes everything", certainly a fundamental concept in the New Sacristy, and the impression of the Divine in its imperturbable essence. Have we here a summary of the universe, an allegory of the vanity of the human world, an enigmatic mockery of the ambitions of the Medici, or a transfiguration of the themes suggested by Pope Clement into a more subtle sphere? Whatever the answer may be, one thing is certain, and contemporaries such as Vasari noticed it: here the freedom and adventure of modern art was born, here "ropes and chains have been severed". It is enough to point out new architectural forms: strange tabernacles above the doors, uneven windows, hollows in the walls, all set in contrast to the basically traditional framework of the whole. And powerful statues, with ever new and wondrous proportions, new expressions and forms of a disconcerting and complex beauty.

The Chapel of the Princes, although already conceived at the time of Cosimo I, was not built until the rule of Ferdinand I in 1604, and its effect is very different. The taste of the seventeenth century was based on the idea of "wonder", but this was expressed through entirely external means. The intention was to build an enormous chapel which would reflect the pomp

San Lorenzo, church of the Medici family.

105

and wealth of the Medici grand-dukes who, although no longer politically powerful, still had ambitions as patrons of art. So we have a mausoleum covered in semi-precious stones, very expensive and delicately carved, an even more sumptuous altar, and enormous tombs also of precious materials; there had even been plans to line the underground passages with precious stones which would glow in the dark, or of stealing the Holy Sepulchre from Jerusalem in order to place it in the centre of the chapel and to attract the masses of pilgrims to Florence. Designs were invited from all the leading architects, but the task was eventually given to Don Giovanni dei Medici, Ferdinand's brother, perhaps because they thought that by hiring a princely architect the result would be more noble. The completion of the work took a long time, and in fact when the Medici died out in the eighteenth century the chapel was still not finished. The Chapel of the Princes was admired throughout the Baroque period, and is still very impressive; but already in 1754 Bottari wrote that the decoration of the chapel was reminiscent of Harlequin's costume; Mengs, who had been asked to decorate the domed ceiling of the chapel and refused, advised that it shoud be closed to the public in respect for the rest of the church; in 1855 Burckhardt wrote of its "clumsy magnificence". Ferdinand had said on the day work began, "Here will be our end", and all the grand-dukes and their families were buried here. The tombs have since been opened and violated many times, both by thieves and by scientists.

Patrons to the end

The Medici had also intended that Michelangelo should build the facade of San Lorenzo. When the artist received the commission in 1516, he made very grand plans (there were to be 22 statues and 7 bas-reliefs), and imagined that it would be "the mirror of architecture and sculpture for the whole of Italy". He spent three years collecting materials in the quarries of Serravezza, but in the end the project was abandoned. The facade was never begun; but having seen some of the facades which were added later to churches in Florence, such as the Cathedral or Santa Croce, the Florentines, like Michelangelo, prefer it "unfinished".

Clement VII did succeed in making Michelangelo build the library of San Lorenzo and its vestibule. The work was begun in 1524 and the library was to house the precious Medici collection, which had been entrusted to the Dominicans of San Marco in 1494 when the Medici were exiled from the city. The two rooms, which were not quite completed when Michelangelo left Florence in 1534, were finished by Vasari and Ammannati under the patronage of Cosimo I and under the guidance of Michelangelo in his voluntary exile in Rome.

The Medici's love for San Lorenzo lasted until the end. The last member of the family, old Anna Maria Ludovica, who ruled from 1737 to 1743, also had plans for finishing the facade of the Chapel of the Princes; she did have the dome of the church frescoed by Meucci, the ceiling of the nave gilded, the underground passages restored, and the bell-tower built' by the architect Ruggieri. But when she too had been buried in San Lorenzo, her successors the Lorraines, despite the instructions in her will, suspended the works. It was not until almost a century later that work was begun again on the church, but the era when, the Medici could discuss projects for their church with architects of the stature of a Brunelleschi or of a Michelangelo was over.

Anna Maria Ludovica dei Medici, the last member of the family, who left her family's artistic treasures to the city.

(illustrations
from page 127 to page 136)

Dante's Florence

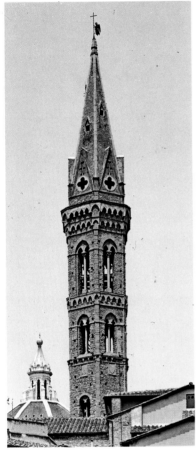

*Bell-tower of the Badia
(thirteenth-fourteenth
centuries).*

*Codice Rustici
Fifteenth-century Ms.,
Badia.*

Dante was born in the spring of 1265 in the heart of Florence, somewhere in the narrow streets between Via Calzaioli and Via del Proconsolo, probably in the area where there is now a group of houses which once belonged to the Alighieri family, rebuilt rather than restored in 1910. His family belonged to the small group of Guelph nobility, but were not very rich; it seems that his father may have helped the family finances along by practising usury. The young Dante nevertheless grew up as a gentleman and received a good education, first from the Franciscan friars in Santa Croce and later in Bologna. When he was 24 years old, in 1289, he took part in the fierce battle of Campaldino against the city of Arezzo; and in 1294 he was probably among the knights chosen by the Commune to honour the Angevin prince, Charles. Sometime around 1295 Dante married Gemma Donati, a neighbour, in the church near his home of San Martino al Vescovo. This church later became the centre of the Compagnia dei Buonomini (Company of Good Men), founded in 1444 by St. Antoninus as a charitable organization as is illustrated in the frescoes, the work of Ghirlandaio's workshop. On the other side of this same square was the proud Torre della Castagna, the first residence of the Priors of the Guilds, who were housed in this fortified tower 'so that they should have nothing to fear from the powerful'. Also close to the Alighieri houses, in the Via Santa Margherita, is the church of the same name, where the Portinari family were buried, one of whom Beatrice (d. 1290), was the woman who inspired Dante's love and his poetry. Beatrice, or Bice, was the daughter of Folco Portinari who owned property nearby, on the Via del Corso, on the spot where the Salviati Palace was built in the fifteenth and sixteenth centuries.

On the day of the Feast of St. John the race of the 'berbers', that is horses without riders, took place along the Corso, running through Florence from east to west. Montaigne recalls seeing this event, but did not find it very entertaining because all he could see was 'horses galloping wildly up a narrow street'. At its eastern end, the Corso crosses Via del Proconsolo and, as one walks towards it, one sees opposite each other two splendid palaces: the Palazzo Nonfinito (Unfinished Palace), built in the sixteenth and seventeenth centuries by Buontalenti, Scamozzi and Cigoli, and the fifteenth-century Pazzi Palace, built by the same family who organised the famous conspiracy against the Medici. It is also worthwhile to take a look at some of the palaces on Borgo degli Albizzi, the street opposite the Corso, among which the one belonging to the Alessandri, a noble family who in the eighteenth century owned an English horse called 'The Great Devil', famous for winning many races in the Corso. But afterwards one must return to the Via del Proconsolo and walk south towards river, where one can see the same buildings familiar to Dante: the Badia and the Bargello.

The Badia was founded before the year 1000, but was rebuilt in 1285, perhaps by Arnolfo di Cambio; its delicate bell-tower was built in 1330. The interior of the church was entirely remodelled in 1627, but the original wall of the apse is still visible today from the Via del Proconsolo. It is said that it was in this church that Boccaccio gave his public lectures on the *Divine Comedy*. As for the Bargello, it already existed before the Palazzo Vecchio was built, as the seat of the Podestà (ruler of the city), with its massive tower called Volognana. In 1266, when Dante was still an infant, a famous chess champion, the Arab Bucceccha, performed there before the Ghibelline Podestà, Count Guido Novello, in matches played 'in the head', that is without seeing the chessboard. The following year, 1267, some prisoners of war were locked up in the tower, which started the long tradition of torture and execution that made the building infamous and a symbol of terror until

1786, when Peter Leopold of Lorraine abolished the death sentence and all forms of torture. A painting now in the Museum of the Bargello portrays the fire in the courtyard of the palace in which all the instruments of torture and execution were publicly burnt. Finally in 1858, when it had ceased to be a prison, the Bargello was restored by the architect Mazzei and transformed into a museum.

Built in the thirteenth century, in the fourteenth century the palace was enlarged: the courtyard was rebuilt with the loggia on the first floor in 1219. The great hall on the first floor, which had been built in 1254 with a trussed ceiling, was now enlarged and given a vaulted ceiling by one of the architects of the Cathedral, Neri di Fioravante. The Chapel was also built at this time and decorated with frescoes by Giotto's school: there is traditionally supposed to be a portrait of Dante in the scene representing Paradise. The palace was severely damaged by fire in 1332, was flooded by the Arno in 1333, and was besieged and taken in 1343 when the Duke of Athens was expelled from Florence. The painter Giottino was commissioned to paint the Duke and his counsellors, and insulting lines were written underneath their portraits. This tradition of portraying political enemies continued into the fourteenth century: from Dante onwards, the Florentines have always been political in their art, and artistic in their politics.

There is a slight confusion, however, between the executions which took place in the Bargello (the police headquarters) when it was still in the Palazzo Vecchio and those which happened in this actual building, which housed the Bargello only after the middle of the sixteenth century. At this time the entire building was turned into a prison; even the grand hall on the first floor, where the meetings of the Council had previously been held, was converted into cells. At any rate, we know that executions took place in this palace as early as 1478, after the Pazzi conspiracy. Four centuries later the Bargello had been transformed into a peaceful museum, housing statues by Donatello, Michelangelo and Cellini, decorated with the vast Carrand collection of minor arts as well as some original Florentine pieces, to which in 1906 the tapestries of Baron Franchetti were added. In fact, as a National Museum, the Bargello is as complete as the Uffizi is as a gallery of painting. The only section which is there now to remind us of the building's past is the collection of armour: this consists of what is left of the splendid Medicean armoury, part of which was sold by the pacifist Peter Leopold, and those pieces belonging to the Ressman collection, acquired in 1899.

Santa Croce Cimabue, Crucifix. Before and after the flood of November 4, 1966.

From the Bargello we cross Piazza San Firenze, with the Gondi Palace built by Giuliano da Sangallo and the beautiful Baroque complex of San Firenze. Turning left, down Borgo dei Greci, we reach Piazza dei Peruzzi, a little island of the Middle Ages with the house of the great Florentine bankers of the thirteenth and fourteenth centuries, mentioned by Dante who calls them 'those of the pear' from the symbol on their coat-of-arms. Some of these houses have curved facades following the contours of the old Roman amphitheatre. The Peruzzi were wealthy enough to have King Robert of Anjou as a guest in their house in 1310; and even after their notorious bankruptcy in 1343 they entertained the Eastern Emperor John VIII Palaeologus. From here we reach the church of Santa Croce, passing through the square where many sermons were preached (those of St Bernadino of Siena were particularly famous), where heretical objects were burnt, where jousts and games took place. Dante knew the first and modest church of Santa Croce, which stood from 1228 till 1292, and saw the beginnings of the new grandiose basilica (1295), which was so splendid that Ubertino da Casale, an adherent of the Spiritualist movement, denounced its excessive luxury in 1310, as a sign of the Anti-Christ. He also condemned the *curiositas picturarum*, referring to the frescoes which decorated the chapels. A popular preacher, the hermit Fidati, was later to claim that the flood of the Arno in 1333 had come as reprisal against the excessive magnificence of this church. But the conflict was won by the guardians of the church who, like the Dominicans in Santa Maria Novella, wanted a church great and large enough to attract the masses of the faithful. The conflict was also won by the rich citizens, the Peruzzi, Bardi, Alberti and Baroncelli families, who competed against each other in building their sumptuous chapels in the new church. The attribution of the architectural plan to the great Arnolfo di Cambio is not an improbable one; there is quality and coherence in the interior space, unified by the arches and the trussed wooden roof, and in the austere beauty of the exterior (apart from the mediocre 1863 facade), with its rhythmical pinnacles and compact polygonal apse. Even the neo-Gothic bell-tower of 1842 is a fair piece of architecture. In the fifteenth century the beauty of the church was further enhanced by Brunelleschi's Pazzi Chapel, by buildings by Michelozzo, and a splendid second courtyard in the style of Brunelleschi.

Santa Croce is both a museum and a pantheon of Florentine great and famous men; at times the two things merge, as in the monuments in honour of great figures, which are also works of art. Two harmonious and decorative tombs which were to serve as prototypes for the Renaissance period are those of Leonardo Bruni, a Humanist and Chancellor of the Republic, designed by Rossellino in 1447, and that of Carlo Marsuppini, also a Humanist and Bruni's successor as Chancellor, by Desiderio da Settignano (1464). In the chapels of the transept we find a unique anthology of Florentine painting of the fourteenth century: late Giotto frescoes in the Bardi and Peruzzi Chapels, illustrating the life of St. Francis; frescoes by Taddeo Gaddi, Giotto's most famous pupil, in the Baroncelli Chapel, painted between 1330 and 1335; Bernardo Daddi in the Pulci-Berardi Chapel (1330); Maso di Banco in the Bardi di Vernio Chapel (1340s); Giovanni da Milano in the Rinuccini Chapel in the sacristy (1365); Agnolo Gaddi, Taddeo's son, in the apse (1390), where, over the altar, there hangs a Crucifix by the Master of Figline. The left aisle of the church was decorated with a *Triumph of Death* and a *Hell* by Orcagna (what is left of this is now kept in the church museum). The stained-glass windows, for the most part designed by these same masters, are also of considerable importance. As for the monuments to the great men who are buried here, we need only mention Ghiberti, Galileo, Machiavelli, Michelangelo, Alfieri (by Canova), Foscolo and Rossini. Dante, whose body has remained in Ravenna, is honoured here with a colossal nineteenth-century monument, the best part of which is perhaps the inscription, in the poet's own words: 'Honour the highest poet'. On the occasion of the sixth centenary of his birth, in 1865, another monument to Dante was built in the centre of the square and has recently been moved to the corner of the church. But really Dante does not need monuments in his own city: with his penetrating intelligence, with his temperament open to all emotions, from fierce wrath to warm love, and ecstatic contemplation, his spirit still lives in the heart of every Florentine.

Telemaco Signorini, Carnival in Piazza Santa Croce. The Franciscan church before the nineteenth-century facade was added.

The Neighbourhood of Via Tornabuoni

Between Piazza Santa Trinita and Piazza Antinori lies the most elegant street of Florence. Until the beginning of the last century the part between Piazza Antinori and Palazzo Strozzi was called Via Larga dei Legnaiuoli (street of the woodworkers), not from the name of an ancient family, but from the many workshops along it, now replaced by elegant shops. In the famous engravings of views of Florence by Zocchi (eighteenth century) the beauty of the street is already apparent. Starting with the part near the elegant Bridge of Santa Trinita we see on the right the imposing Palazzo Spini (later Feroni) which dates from around 1290, built by Messer Geri degli Spini, a veteran of the battle of Campaldino and an important political and economical figure, who could afford to have this great private castle constructed. It is crowned by medieval battlements and has clusters of little windows on the three upper floors. Originally the street along the river did not exist, so the left side of the palace and its tower dominated the river. The appearance of the palace today is the result of a restoration in the nineteenth century.

On the other side of the street, the church of Santa Trinita has a very extravagant, almost proto-Baroque facade, built in 1593 by Buontalenti. The interior, on the other hand, is very severe thirteenth-century Gothic style but its chapels reflect the wealth and the taste of the great families of the parish. The Bartolini-Salimbeni Chapel, for instance, is one of the few remaining examples of a late-Gothic chapel (1423), with its unified decoration, from the wrought iron gate to the frescoes and altarpiece by Lorenzo Monaco. In the Sacristy (built between 1418 and 1423, probably on a design by Ghiberti), commissioned by the Strozzi, there were works by Gentile da Fabriano (his *Adoration of the Magi* today at the Uffizi was painted for this sacristy) and Donatello; then there is the Renaissance Sassetti Chapel with the cycle of the *Life of St. Francis* by Ghirlandaio (1483-86), in which we can see, apart from portraits of many Florentine officials of the time, including Lorenzo the Magnificent, a view of Piazza Santa Trinita as it was at the time, the facade of the church decorated with Romanesque arches.

In the square there is the Column of Justice, erected by Cosimo I dei Medici in 1565; the column itself was brought from Caracalla's Baths in Rome. Opposite is the Palazzo Bartolini, built in 1523 on a design by Baccio d'Agnolo and subject to much criticism at the time. The works are well documented in a book kept by the Bartolini family, as was the custom among all Florentine noblemen, where the expenses for the construction were all recorded. Palazzo Bartolini, with its great pedimented windows flanked by niches, succeeds in preserving the traditional characteristics of Florentine palace architecture in the style of the sixteenth century. The architect nearly went mad with all the attacks that he was subjected to; he replied with the inscription in Latin, that it is easier to criticize than to imitate. The palace deserves its place in history. In the nineteenth century the palace became the fashionable and cosmopolitan Hotel du Nord, among whose guests were Emerson, Melville and Macaulay. Today it is the seat of the French Consulate.

Still very much in the Florentine fifteenth-century style is the facade of the Palazzo Strozzi, begun in 1489 for Filippo Strozzi, who entrusted its construction to Benedetto da Maiano. Strozzi, who had returned to Florence after a long exile in Naples, had for a long time wanted to build himself this palace; since he had had two wives and children from each of them, he wanted the palace to be internally divided into two apartments, which is why the palace has two staircases, etc. He only lived long enough to see the walls built to the height of the rings for tying up horses, but left instructions in his will that it was to be completed. Although the palace imitates the Medici palace, the internal courtyard, built by Cronaca between 1492 and 1503, is on a larger scale, built in the High Renaissance style, worthy of the rich and

Santa Trinita
The Sassetti Chapel with
Ghirlandaio's frescoes.

proud Strozzi family, the fiercest rivals and later the declared enemies of the Medici. When, in the sixteenth century, the clash between the two families reached its climax, the Medici confiscated half of the palace (1538-1568). But the Strozzi were later pardoned and they outlived the Medici and, until the last century, continued to live in the palace where they held splendid celebrations, such as that in 1896 in honour of the King of Italy. In 1907 the palace was offered to the State, which refused to accept it on the grounds that the conditions were too onerous; in 1937 it was bought by the Istituto Nazionale delle Assicurazioni (National Insurance Company) and today it houses many important artistic events of the city.

The Strozzi family, which was divided into many branches, owned several other buildings in this part of the city near the old church of Santa Maria degli Ughi (no longer extant). Among them in the square which today still bears their name, built at great expense and inaugurated in 1533, the Palazzo dello Strozzino, perhaps begun by Michelozzo and finished by Giuliano da Maiano. This palace had a lovely fifteenth-century courtyard, destroyed in 1920 to make room for the Odeon cinema, designed by Piacentini, who later became the architect of the Fascist regime.

The second part of Via Tornabuoni also has some important buildings: the Loggetta dei Tornaquinci by Cigoli (built in the early seventeenth century); the small Palazzo Giacomini attributed to Dosio (1580), whose sobre elegance inspired the architects of the nineteenth-century Florentine villas; and the sombre, fifteenth-century Palazzo Antinori (1461-1469), probably by Giuliano da Maiano. In this building there is a place where one can sample the renowned wines and farm produce of the Antinori estates. The Florentine aristocracy has maintained its economic position, thanks primarily to agricultural produce. Opposite is the seventeenth-century facade of the church of San Gaetano, a work of Silvani, which, although Baroque in style, in based on a Florentine design.

Leaving the Via Tornabuoni, and passing through some narrow streets, we now reach the Dominican basilica of Santa Maria Novella (1246-1360), with its large square built in 1324 where the chariot race used to take place. Santa Maria Novella, with its three naves and its Gothic ribbed vault, flanked by the low Green Cloister, is very different from the "simple", although splendidly decorated, Santa Croce of the Franciscans; its atmosphere is graver, just as the doctrine of the Dominicans was more rigorous than that of the Franciscans. The architects who began work on this church, Fra Sisto and Fra Ristoro, were both Dominicans. Leon Battista Alberti later worked on giving the facade a unified appearance, although one can still clearly distinguish the Romanesque, Gothic and Renaissance parts. The interior contains a few works which would appear in any history of art: Filippino Lippi's frescoes (1502) in the Strozzi Chapel (commissioned by Filippo Strozzi) are exciting and bizarrely theatrical, perhaps inspired by the contemporary Florentine Renaissance masques; in the apse of the main chapel are Ghirlandaio's frescoes (despite their vast scale, executed in only five years, from 1485 to 1490), which illustrate the lives of Mary and St. John the Baptist; in the Gondi Chapel is the remarkable wooden *Crucifix* by Brunelleschi and, in the left transept, Dante's vision of the after-life is illustrated by Nardo di Cione (1357). In the sacristy there is a *Crucifix* by Giotto; finally in the left aisle, is the solemn *Trinity* by Masaccio, the lower part of which was only discovered in 1951 and represents a skeleton, symbolic of Death, with an admonitory inscription: "I once was what you are now; and what I am now, you will be". In the Green Cloister, Paolo Uccello painted his extraordinary fresco cycle of the *Flood* (now detached from the wall); the grandiose Cappellone degli Spagnoli, originally the Chapter House, was frescoed in 1355 by Andrea Bonaiuti with illustrations of doctrinal themes. The convent was once enormous (a large cloister is now occupied by the Carabinieri, a branch of the police), and its gardens extended to where the railway station is today.

If we walk down Via dei Fossi, a street of antique dealers, and reach the Arno at the Ponte alla Carraia, we can see along the river the grandiose

Palace of the Corsini Princes, begun in 1650 by Don Giovanni dei Medici, Cosimo I's illegitimate son, a general and an architect. Inside the palace, which was only completed in 1737, there are splendidly frescoed halls and an important collection of paintings. If we, on the other hand, turn down Via della Vigna Nuova, we can see the Rucellai Palace (1451), built by Rossellino on a project by Alberti. The palace was made for Giovanni Rucellai, whose *Zibaldone*, a collection of notes used for the education of his sons, is a lively source of information about life in fifteenth-century Florence. He was a son-in-law of Palla Strozzi, later exiled by the Medici, but nevertheless managed to marry one of his sons to Lorenzo the Magnificent's sister Nannina. The palace he had built is a masterpiece based on the principles of ancient Roman buildings, the three storeys are clearly marked on the facade and the mullioned windows are emphasized by ornate lintels. The ground floor has stone benches attached to it, a Florentine custom intended to provide resting places for passers-by. At a corner, between two streets, is the Rucellai Loggia, with three arches, which was intended, as Giovanni Rucellai wrote, "for the honour of our family . . . for the joys and the grief". These loggias, used for banquets and feasts or funerals in the presence of the people, or simply as shaded meeting-places, were an annex to all the great houses, whether within the house or very nearby, a symbol of the cordial power of the local oligarchy. It also seems that these loggias were traditionally regarded as places of asylum or protection. Later, however, the wealthy retired into the privacy of their houses and gardens, and the loggias became workshops.

The tour of the neighbourhood of Via Tornabuoni can be concluded with a visit to Palazzo Davanzati (originally the palace of the Davizzi family), a great fourteenth-century construction which was ably restored in 1906 by the antiquarian Volpi, and converted into the museum of the Florentine home. Here we can see all the details, the courtyard, the stairs, the well, the frescoed rooms with tapestries and curtains, the fireplaces, the bathrooms, which comprised the typical interior of the palace of a prosperous Florentine merchant.

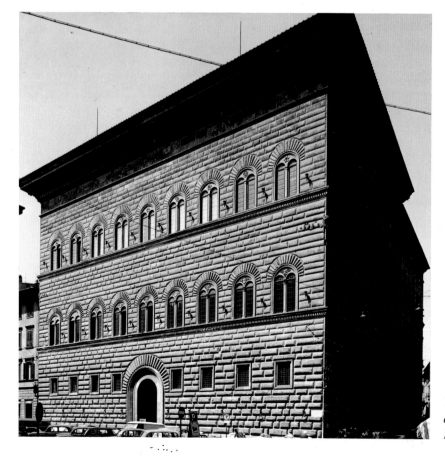

The Strozzi Palace, designed by Benedetto da Maiano.

Medici Museum
Agnolo Bronzino,
Giovanni di Bicci de' Medici.
Posthumous portrait of the
founder of the dynasty
which ruled over Florence
and Tuscany.

Medici Museum
Agnolo Bronzino,
Cosimo the Elder.
Founder of the family
fortune
and great patron of the arts.

London, National Gallery
Agnolo Bronzino,
Piero the Gouty.
Son of Cosimo and father of
Lorenzo the Magnificent,
Piero commissioned many
great works of art including
the Gozzoli frescoes.

Medici Museum
Agnolo Bronzino,
Lorenzo the Magnificent.
A poet, a shrewd political
thinker and a great patron of
the arts, Lorenzo was until
his death (1492) responsible
for preserving
the equilibrium among
the Italian states.

Medici Museum
Agnolo Bronzino,
Giuliano de' Medici.
Lorenzo's brother,
who was killed in the
Pazzi conspiracy (1478).

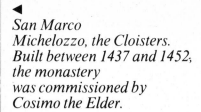

San Marco
Michelozzo, the Cloisters.
Built between 1437 and 1452,
the monastery
was commissioned by
Cosimo the Elder.

Michelozzo, the Library.
A refined fifteenth-century
construction, this room still
shows a certain Gothic
influence.

Fra Angelico,
Musician Angel.
Detail from
the Linaiuoli tabernacle,
painted in 1433-34.

▶

Fra Angelico,
Burial of Saints Cosmas and
Damian (detail).
This panel was part of the
predella of the altarpiece of
San Marco, painted for the
high altar of the church
towards 1440.

Fra Angelico,
Annunciation.
This fresco, one of
Angelico's most famous
works,
is at the top of the stairs that
lead to the cells of the
monastery.

Fra Angelico, the Damned
(detail from
the Last Judgment).

Fra Angelico, the Blessed
(detail from
the Last Judgment).
These two details are part
of the scene of
the Last Judgment,
painted in 1430 for
Santa Maria degli Angeli.

*Medici-Riccardi Palace
Benozzo Gozzoli,
The Procession of the Magi
(panel with Lorenzo
the Magnificent).*

*Benozzo Gozzoli,
The Procession of the Magi,
 detail .*

*Benozzo Gozzoli,
The Procession of the Magi
(panel with the Emperor
John Palaeologus).
In this elaborate cycle of
frescoes, Gozzoli portrayed
the important people who
took part in the Council of
Florence (1439) and in Pope
Pius II's journey to Florence
(1459). The frescoes are in
the chapel of the palace.*

*San Lorenzo,
the interior.
The church, which is said to
have been founded by Saint
Ambrose, was rebuilt
according to plans by
Brunelleschi and finished in
1460.
It was the first church in
Florence to be built in
Renaissance style.*

*San Lorenzo
Donatello,
Resurrection and Ascension.*

*Donatello,
Crucifixion and Deposition
from the Cross.
Bas-reliefs from Donatello's
two pulpits, both in the
church of San Lorenzo.*

▲
San Lorenzo
Donatello,
Christ resurrected
(detail of the pulpit).
The anguish of this figure is
typical of Donatello's
dramatic realism.

San Lorenzo,
Old Sacristy.
This sacristy was designed
and built
by Brunelleschi
between 1422 and 1428.

San Lorenzo,
Chapel of the Princes.
This sacristy, lavishly
decorated with semi-precious
stones and rare marble,
contains the tombs of the
Medici grand-dukes.

▶
San Lorenzo,
New Sacristy.
Designed by Michelangelo,
this room houses the tombs
of several members of the
Medici family. On the right
we can see the monument to
Giuliano, Duke of Nemours.

◀
*San Lorenzo,
New Sacristy
Michelangelo,
Twilight and Dawn.
These two statues
decorate the tomb of
Lorenzo, Duke of Urbino.*

▶

*Michelangelo,
Monument to
Giuliano, Duke of Nemours.*

Michelangelo, Night (detail).

*Michelangelo,
Lorenzo, Duke of Urbino
(detail).*

Michelangelo, Dawn (detail).

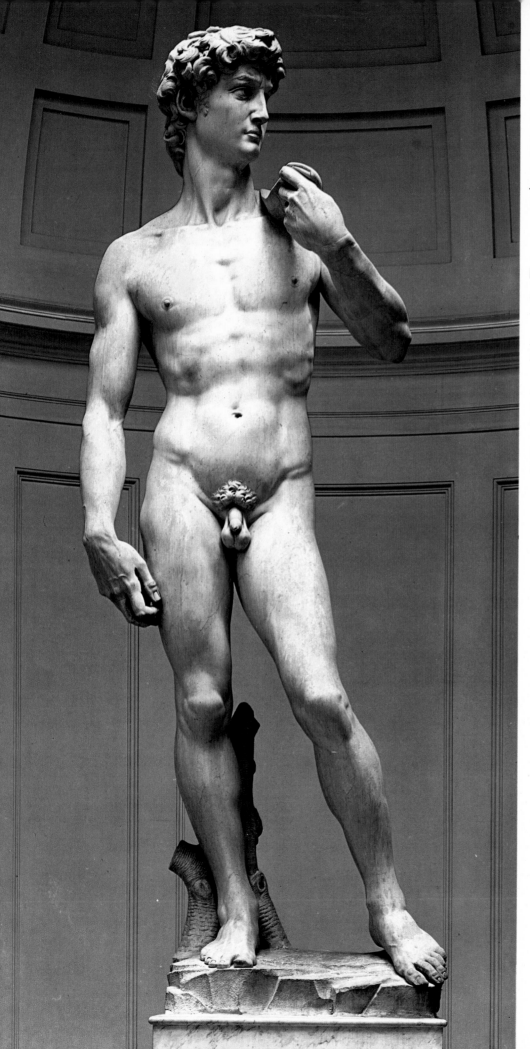

◀
Academy of Fine Arts
Michelangelo, David.
The artist sculpted this figure
between 1501 and 1504 using
a piece of marble which had
been discarded by the
fifteenth-century artist
Agostino di Duccio.

▶

Michelangelo, David.
Detail of the hand.

Michelangelo, David.
Detail of the head.

Michelangelo, Prisoner.
One of the statues
commonly known as
'prisoners', which were to
have decorated the tomb of
Pope Julius II.

◀
Academy of Fine Arts
Michelangelo, two Prisoners.

▶
Archeological Museum
Vase known as 'François'.
(from the name of the
archeologist who discovered
it).
This vase was painted in the
sixth century B.C. by the
Athenian Klithias and was
found in an Etruscan tomb.

'Chimera'
Etruscan bronze sculpture of
the sixth century B.C.

Etruscan vase in the shape
of a bull.

The orator.
Bronze statue from the
second century B.C.,
Etruscan but already under
Roman influence.

Santissima Annunziata
Unknown fourteenth-century
artist, Annunciation.
One of the most famous
devotional paintings in
Florence which,
according to legend,
was painted by an angel.

Santissima Annunziata
Andrea del Castagno,
Holy Trinity.
One of the last works of this
powerful Florentine painter
(1454-55).

Hospital of the Innocents,
Museum
Luca della Robbia,
Madonna and Child.
In glazed terracotta,
this is a typical work of
Luca's.

▶

Torre della Castagna
This tower is in the oldest
part of the city, across from
where Dante's house was;
the Guilds used to meet here
before the Palazzo Vecchio
was built.

Piazza Peruzzi
In the curve of this old
building we can still
distinguish the outline of the
Roman amphitheatre.

Torre degli Alberti
A perfect example of the
medieval tower-house, it was
built for the aristocratic
family of the Alberti; one
can still see their emblem,
crossed chains, on the
capitals of the columns.

National Museum (Bargello)
School of Giotto,
Portrait of Dante.
This is a detail of a fresco of
the Last Judgement in the
chapel of the Bargello.

Dante's House
This building has been
heavily restored but it stands
on the spot where Dante's
family owned some
buildings.

◄
*Michelangelo's House
(Casa Buonarroti)
Michelangelo,
Madonna 'della Scala',
detail.
Perhaps the earliest of
Michelangelo's works to
have come down to us, it is
usually dated around 1490.*

*Michelangelo,
Battle of the Centaurs, detail.
Sculpted in 1492, when the
artist was seventeen.*

*Santa Croce, facade.
A modern addition (1853-63)
to the magnificent
Franciscan church.*

►

*Santa Croce, apse.
A general view of the area
around the high altar, with
the polyptych by
Niccolò Gerini and Giovanni
del Biondo
(end of the fourteenth
century), the Crucifix by the
'Master of Figline',
and the frescoes by
Agnolo Gaddi.*

*Santa Croce
Tomb of Michelangelo.
There are many tombs
of famous men in the
church.
Michelangelo's was designed
by Vasari (1570) and
carried
out by contemporary
painters and sculptors.*

*Stefano Ricci,
Dante's Cenotaph.
A Neoclassical artist,
Ricci sculpted this
monument in memory of the
great poet who was buried in
Ravenna.*

*Tomb of Galileo.
The Florentine scientist
was buried in this tomb
designed by Foggini. To the
right is the personification of
Geometry, to the left
Astronomy.*

GALILAEVS GALILEIVS PATRIC. FLOR.

129

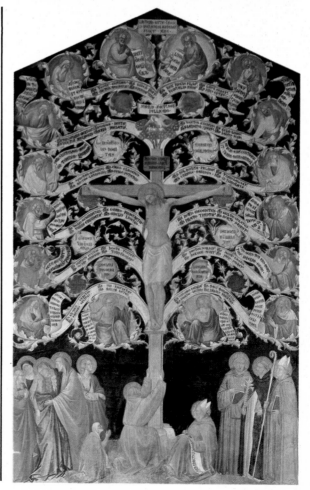

◄
Santa Croce
Benedetto da Maiano,
Death of St. Francis
and Fortitude.
Two details of the pulpit
which is considered the
masterpiece of this
fifteenth-century artist.

Donatello, Annunciation.
One of the master's rare
works in 'pietra serena' with
gold highlights (c. 1435).

Giovanni da Milano,
Expulsion of Joachim from
the Temple.
A detail of the wonderful
frescoes by this
north Italian painter,
active in Florence in
the second half of the
fourteenth century, which
decorate the
Rinuccini Chapel
in the Sacristy.

Taddeo Gaddi,
The Tree of the Cross.
Painted in the refectory
(now the museum),
it is the work of Giotto's
closest follower.

►
Giotto,
Death of St. Francis.
One of the frescoes depicting
the story of St. Francis
which cover the walls of
the Bardi Chapel

Giotto,
Apparition of St. Francis.
Detail of a monk looking
out from behind a curtain.

Giotto, Trial by fire.
Detail of the Sultan, from
another episode from
the life of St. Francis
in the Bardi Chapel.

◄
Santa Croce
Filippo Brunelleschi,
Pazzi Chapel, interior.
This building was planned by
Brunelleschi, but he died
before he could finish it.

Filippo Brunelleschi,
Pazzi Chapel, facade.

Glazed terracotta roundel,
St. Matthew.
Glazed terracotta roundel,
St. John the Evangelist.
These roundels with the
Evangelists decorate the
inside spandrels of
the Pazzi Chapel;
they are the work of
Luca della Robbia.

►
National Museum (Bargello)
Internal courtyard.
The most impressive part of
the city's first public palace,
the seat of the Podestà,
of the Captains of the
People and later of the
police.

Giuseppe Zocchi,
The Bargello (etching).
One of the views of Florence
published by Zocchi in 1744.

1

2

3

4

5

6

7

8

9

10

11

12

13

National Museum (Bargello)
1. Donatello, St. George.
This statue (1416) used to be
in the tabernacle of
the Armourers and
Swordmakers Guild in
Orsanmichele.

2. Andrea della Robbia,
Portrait of a girl.

3. Giambologna, Mercury.

4. Gianlorenzo Bernini,
Portrait
of Costanza Bonarelli.

5. Andrea della Robbia,
Portrait of a boy.

6. Francesco Laurana,
Portrait of
Battista Sforza.

7. Giambologna, Turkey.

8. Donatello, David.
Sculpted around 1430
for Cosimo the Elder, this
statue was the first nude of
the Renaissance.

9. Michelangelo,
Bacchus.

10. Andrea del Verrocchio,
David.
A bronze statue by the
Florentine sculptor and
painter who was Leonardo's
teacher.

11. The 'Lamina di Agilulfo'.
One of the rare pieces of
barbarian art in Italy, it
portrays the Lombard king
Agilulf between two angels.

12. Michelangelo,
Madonna and Child
with St. John (Pitti Tondo).

13. Armour of Charles V.
Sophisticated sixteenth-
century craftsmanship,
probably from a Milanese
armoury.

Bardini Museum
A remarkable collection of
antiques, left to the city
by Stefano Bardini.

Piazza Santa Croce,
Palazzo Antellesi.
One of the rare Florentine
palaces that still retains its
fresco decoration on the
facade.

Palazzo Gondi, Courtyard.
Designed by
Giuliano da Sangallo,
this is a wonderful example
of Renaissance architecture
(1490-1501).

Horne Museum
Giotto, St. Stephen.
This panel was once part of
a polyptych which has been
dismembered;
it dates from 1320-25.

Horne Museum
A precious collection of
works of art, it was donated
to the Italian State
by the art historian
Herbert P. Horne
in 1919.

*Piazza Santa Trinita.
One of the most lovely
squares of the city, it is
surrounded by buildings
of artistic and historic
interest, such as
Palazzo Spini Ferroni
(in the background)
and Palazzo
Bartolini Salimbeni
(on the left).
In the centre is the column
with the statue of Justice,
brought here from Rome
by Cosimo I.*

*Santa Trinita
Domenico Ghirlandaio,
Adoration of the
Shepherds.In the Sassetti
Chapel,
this painting clearly shows
the importance of Flemish
influence on Florentine
painting of the second half
of the fifteenth century.*

*Domenico Ghirlandaio,
Adoration of the Shepherds.
 detail .*

*Santa Trinita
Luca della Robbia,
Tomb of Bishop
Benozzo Federighi. 1450.*

◀
Santa Maria Novella.
The lower part of the facade
dates from the first half of
the fourteenth century; the
upper part was designed by
Leon Battista Alberti (1470),
who continued the
traditionally Florentine
colour scheme.

Masaccio, Trinity.
The architectural
construction which encloses
the scene was almost
certainly suggested by
Brunelleschi.

Domenico Ghirlandaio,
Birth of John the Baptist.
This is one of the frescoes in
the apse of the church,
commissioned by
theTornabuoni family (1485-
90).
Here we see two details.

Filippino Lippi,
St. Philip exorcises the
monster.
One of the frescoes of the
cycle which illustrates the life
of St. Philip, in the Strozzi
Chapel (1497-1502).

Andrea Buonaiuti,
The Militant Church (detail).
This fresco, in the
Cappellone degli Spagnoli,
shows what must have been
Arnolfo's project for the
dome of the Cathedral.

▶
Church of Ognissanti
Sandro Botticelli,
St. Augustine.
Painted for this Franciscan
church in 1480.

Palazzo Davanzati,
Sala dei Pappagalli.
(Room of the Parrots).
Typical fourteenth-century
room in a Florentine palace
belonging to a rich merchant
family.

◀

*Ponte Santa Trinita,
Destroyed by German bombs
in 1944, this bridge was
rebuilt according to
Ammannati's original
designs. In the background,
the Ponte Vecchio, built in
the fourteenth century.*

*'Firenze com'era'
Museum
Giuseppe Moricci,
The Arno with
the Ponte Vecchio.
Nineteenth-century painting
of one of the most
characteristic views of
Florence.*

*Gallery of Modern Art
Antonio Fontanesi,
The Arno.
Typically Romantic painting
with the Ponte Vecchio and
Ponte Santa Trinita.*

*London, British Museum
J. M. W. Turner, Florence.*

▶

*Santa Maria del Carmine,
Brancacci Chapel
Masaccio,
The Tribute.
The central part of the most
famous fresco by the
founder of Florentine
Renaissance painting (1425-
27).*

*Masaccio
Distribution of Alms.*

Santa Maria del Carmine,
Brancacci Chapel
Masaccio,
St. Peter healing the sick
with his shadow (detail).
Masaccio's characters
portray the new Renaissance
man with all his dignity.

Masaccio,
The Fall (detail).

Filippino Lippi,
Self-portrait.
The son of Filippo Lippi, he
was given the task of
finishing the frescoes in the
Brancacci Chapel in 1481.

Masaccio,
Baptism of the Neophytes
(detail).
This shivering nude is
Masaccio's most powerful
creation.

▶
Via Toscanella
A typical street
in the Santo Spirito
neighbourhood.

San Frediano in Cestello

Santo Spirito,
The bare sixteenth-century
facade completes
Brunelleschi's church.

Santo Spirito
Unknown fifteenth-century
artist, Madonna of Succour.

Santo Spirito, Filippino
Lippi, Nerli Altarpiece
(detail showing Porta San
Frediano).

Santa Felicita
Pontormo, Deposition.

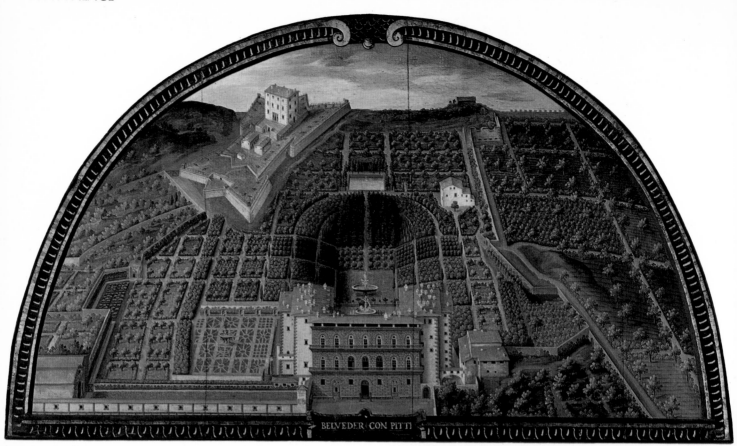

BELVEDER CON PITTI

Justus Utens, Pitti Palace and the Boboli Gardens. This lunette is one of a series depicting Medici palaces and villas; it was painted in 1599.

Pitti Palace, facade. Begun by Brunelleschi for Luca Pitti, this building was later bought by Eleonor of Toledo and became the seat of the Medici grand dukes.

▶

Pitti Palace Palatine Gallery Titian, Concert. Until recently this painting was attributed sometimes to Titian and sometimes to Giorgione.

Rubens, the four Philosophers.

▶▶

Following pages: Palatine Gallery Raphael, The veiled Woman.

Murillo, Madonna and Child.

Andrea del Sarto, St. John the Baptist.

Raphael, Madonna 'of the Grand Duke'.

Raphael, Madonna 'of the Chair'.

RAFFAELLO SANZIO
N. AD URBI O 6 A RILE 1483
M. A ROMA 6 APRILE 1520
MADONNA .... SEGGIOLA

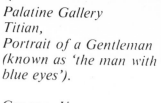

*Palatine Gallery
Titian,
Portrait of a Gentleman
(known as 'the man with
blue eyes').*

Canova, Venus.

Guido Reni, Young Bacchus.

*Pietro da Cortona,
Golden Age
(fresco in the
Stanza della Stufa).*

*Caravaggio,
Sleeping Cupid.*

*Museo degli Argenti
Jasper vase, made in Venice.
It used to belong to
Lorenzo the Magnificent.*

*Florentine workshop,
Cosimo II in prayer.*

*German workshop,
boat-shaped jewel.*

*Bernardino Gaffurri,
Piazza della Signoria
with the statue of Cosimo I.*

◄
*Gallery of Modern Art
Giovanni Fattori, Runaway
Horse.
Dramatic painting by one of
the leaders of the
Macchiaioli school.*

*Boboli Gardens
Valerio Cioli,
the dwarf Morgante.
Bizarre late sixteenth-century
statue of one of the dwarfs
at Cosimo I's court.*

*The Isolotto pond in the
Boboli gardens.*

►

*San Miniato
Facade.
This church, on a hill above
the city, was built in the
thirteenth century and shows
all the characteristics of the
sobre Florentine
Romanesque style.*

Mosaic in the apse.

*Belvedere fortress.
Built after a project by
Bernardo Buontalenti, it was
intended more as protection
against insurrections than
against invasions.*

*View of Florence from
Piazzale Michelangelo.*

The Arno, Oltrarno, Pitti and Boboli

It has been pointed out that the river Arno changes as it flows through Florence: it enters the city from the east, still with the fresh quickness of a torrent coming from the mountains; it leaves the city near the park of the Cascine, to the west, much more sluggish, almost as though it could already feel the sea (still eighty kilometres away). At times blue, at times yellow and muddy, at times practically dry, at times swollen and menacing (besides the flood of November 4th 1966, there have been many other disastrous ones in the history of the city, such as the one in 1333, also on November 4th, that of 1547, and the one on November 3rd 1844), the Arno is as changeable as the Florentine temperament. The city, for its own part, has exploited and polluted the river ever since the beginning, using it for the tanning of leather, for the dyeing of wool and cloth, and as supply of water and sand. Even today the river is not treated well. The Arno was also used for certain celebrations, for the amusement of the wealthy (as can be seen in eighteenth-century paintings); and an old photograph shows a musical café anchored opposite Palazzo Corsini.

Of the bridges which span the river, the Ponte Vecchio is as old as the city itself; its present structure dates from 1345, after the previous bridge had been washed away by the 1333 flood. The first shops had been built as early as the thirteenth century and housed leather tanneries, then butchers and costermongers, until the Grand-Duke Ferdinand I, in 1593, banned these "base arts", reserving it for goldsmiths and jewellers. During the German retreat of 1944, the bridge — over which Hitler had crossed the river in the Vasari Corridor, during his visit to the Florentine museums in 1938 — was spared, unlike all the others. And it also withstood the 1966 flood, although the debris of trees and cars carried by the waters struck it like battering-rams. Upstream, the Ponte alle Grazie (blown up in 1944) dated from 1237 and, above its pilasters, housed little chapels (one dedicated to the Madonna delle Grazie gave the bridge its name). Originally it had a nine arch span.

Downstream, the Ponte Santa Trinita (1570) has been called by a German critic "the most beautiful bridge in the world", and it was thought to have been designed by Michelangelo. But its clearly defined intellectual elegance is not the work of Michelangelo, who at that time had already emigrated to the more monumental Rome; it is a purely Florentine work, of that great architect Ammannati. This bridge is not only an aesthetic masterpiece, but also a technical and functional one; Ammannati was in fact replacing a previous bridge, twice destroyed by floods. The sharp edge of its supporting pylons was designed to break the impact of debris carried by the flood-waters, and its high arches provide an outlet for great masses of water. The roadway is, on the other hand, very slender, completed by elegant marble ornaments at the centre of each of the three sections. Despite this slenderness, the bridge gave proof of its solidity at the beginning of the nineteenth century, when the French crossed it with all their heavy artillery. The German mines destroyed it in 1944, but is was reconstructed exactly as "it had been", despite a fierce debate, which happily dismissed the idea of giving it an internal structure of reinforced concrete. The bridge connects the elegant Via Maggio in Oltrarno (the other side of the river from the centre), where the house of Bianca Cappello is, the mistress of Grand-Duke Francesco I.

After flowing through the city for three kilometres, flanked on both sides by the spacious "lungarni" (avenues along the Arno), except for the section next to the Ponte Vecchio, the Arno covers another three kilometres through the park of the Cascine, until its confluence with the torrent Mugnone. In this same spot, in 1870, the young Maharajah Raiaram Cuttraputti, who died in Florence, was cremated and is recalled by a strange, pagoda-shaped monument called *L'Indiano*. In the last century, the park of the Cascine was

Portrait of Benvenuto Cellini by Romanelli (1900), on the Ponte Vecchio.

the setting for Sunday afternoon outings: the carriages of the nobles and the rich, drawn by elegant horses, strolled along the avenues and the ladies showed off their jewellery and their clothes, talking to each other from carriage to carriage, while the less rich were content to look on. Stendhal wrote in 1817: "The Cascine, a promenade where everyone goes to show themselves off, are comparable to the Champs Elysées. Alas, I always find it inhabited by six hundred Russians or Englishmen. Florence is only a museum full of foreigners, enforcing their own customs".

Masaccio at the Carmine

On the first day after his arrival in Florence, Stendhal had gone to see the tombs of the great men in Santa Croce, while re-reading Foscolo's poem *I Sepolcri*, which he had in his attaché-case; the second day he went to the "church of the Carmine where Masaccio's frescoes are". Stendhal's instincts were right, for a visit to see Masaccio's frescoes in the Carmine is an experience beyond that of going to museums and mausoleums, it is a visit to the heart of Florence and to one of the greatest works of art in the city. What we know of Masaccio's life suggests that he eschewed high living and was dedicated only to his art, unlike his great Flemish contemporary, Van Eyck, who acted both as a diplomat and as a courtier in his native Bruges. Masaccio was held in high esteem by such politically important figures as Felice Brancacci, who commissioned this chapel in the Carmine, and later he was called to Rome to work for members of the Holy See. It was there that Masaccio died in 1428 aged 26, either from the plage or from poisoning. At the outset of his career, he had portrayed the consecration of the church of the Carmine in 1422 in the famous fresco called the *Sagra*, formerly in the cloister of that church but destroyed in 1600. The fresco showed the square in front of the church and a great procession of people, amongst whom he included portraits of his friends: Brunelleschi was shown wearing wooden clogs, also Donatello and Masolino (who later collaborated with Masaccio on the Brancacci Chapel). He also portrayed the foremost political figures of the day: Uzzano, Giovanni di Bicci dei Medici, Brancacci and others, and he included the gatekeeper standing with the keys in his hands by the door of the convent. All this was shown with the utmost realism; sadly we only know of the fresco's appearance from copies.

The Brancacci Chapel became the school of the Florentine Renaissance painters, including Michelangelo. Here we shall limit ourselves to pointing out the civic meaning of this cycle, which, as is indicated by the episode of the *Tribute Money*, is obviously a reference to the catasto, the important egalitarian tax reform passed in Florence in 1427. Masaccio was implying that it is necessary to "render unto Caesar that which is Caesar's", i.e. pay one's taxes. He himself made his tax declaration in July 1427, from which we learn that he lived in a rented house with his mother and his younger brother and that he also paid the rent for half a workshop near the Bargello; also he had many debts. At that time this very modest tax-payer was, together with Van Eyck, one of the greatest painters in the world; and no one knows how his painting would have developed if he had not died the following year. Brunelleschi, usually very pungent in his remarks about other artists, this time commented: "We have suffered a great loss".

Typical artisan workshops in Oltrarno.

View of Florence from the Belvedere Fortress during the Henry Moore exhibition.

Palazzo Pitti: the last of the Medici

A visit to the Carmine is a good introduction to the Oltrarno, with its slum streets and its bare squares such as the Piazza del Carmine itself or Piazza Tasso; Piazza Santo Spirito, enlivened by an open market, is much less harsh. Behind a modest facade in this square is Brunelleschi's great basilica, with its magnificent *pietra serena* colonnades, but which basically shares the Roman *dignitas* of Masaccio's figures. Picturesque streets, such as Via del Campuccio and Via Toscanella, artisan workshops of furniture and picture frames, which restore or "create" antiques, and a special vernacular, which distinguishes itself from the Florentine spoken across the river, called "sanfredianino", from the church of San Frediano; this language is very broad, but also traditionally witty and sharp. These are the distinctive traits of this section of the city, working-class (even though there are some noble palaces) and fascinating, full of life, where the essence of old Florence seems to have been best preserved. This zone is much liked by foreigners.

The Oltrarno has its own great monument, the Pitti Palace and its immense garden, the Boboli, enjoyed by all the city. The merchant Luca Pitti, an ambitious and corrupt friend of the Medici's (against whom he later led a conspiracy), ordered the palace to be built in 1458, at the foot of the hill of Boboli. The original plan of the palace was much smaller, the width of the seven central windows of today's palace. But those windows with their immense frames are enough to show us what an ambitious project Luca Pitti had in mind. The plans of this imposing construction were probably drawn up by Brunelleschi; the houses of the poor were ruthlessly knocked down to make room for the building and the square; the enormous blocks of stone used for the facade were excavated from a quarry in the Boboli gardens. Luca Pitti was totally unscrupulous in the methods he used to raise money in order to complete the building; Machiavelli tells us that gifts of money were extorted from everyone, contributions were demanded from local government officials and even prisoners, who were given protection in exchange. In 1549, the palace was sold to Eleonor of Toledo, the wife of Cosimo I, and the imposing and beautiful courtyard was added by Ammannati following the design of great Roman villas, and the gardens were adorned with grottos, statues, fountains and little lakes. In the seventeenth century the facade was widened, and in the eighteenth the two side wings were added. Not even Luca Pitti, for all his ambitions, could have ever imagined the eventual size and the grandeur of the palace he had begun. Taine wrote of the palace: "I do not believe that there is in Europe a more monumental palace; as far as I am concerned, I have never seen another which left such a grand, and such a simple impression on me".

The Pitti Palace with its spacious park, had been bought for reasons of the health of the Duchess Eleonor of Toledo; she had been very strong, but had given Cosimo I eleven children and by 1549 appeared very "worn" as one can see in a portrait by Bronzino in Berlin. It seems, in fact, that she died of tuberculosis. Her sons, Francesco I and Ferdinand I, who succeeded their father, were strong and healthy men, but Cosimo II (1590-1621) was a sickly grand duke who passed his years "between bed and couch", as the contemporary documents put it. Cosimo II was outlived by his mother Cristina of Lorraine and by his wife, Mary Magdalen of Austria, two fat widows, always dressed in black, bigoted and incompetent. Finally Ferdinand II (1610-1670) came of age; he ruled for half a century and gave Florence a period of comparative peace, assisted by his brothers including the extremely intelligent Cardinal Leopold. Cosimo II had already begun the enlargement of the palace (he had the first stone brought to his bed-chamber, where he lay ill, in order to put the mortar on it himself, in 1620); Ferdinand II continued the task and also commissioned the decoration of some of the great halls with frescoes by Giovanni da San Giovanni (1636) and others, with perspective *trompe l'oeil* paintings by Colonna and Mitelli (1636). He also commissioned Pietro da Cortona, the famous Roman Baroque artist, to

Santo Spirito
Alessandro Allori, Predella
(detail of the facade of the Pitti Palace in the sixteenth century).

paint the frescoes on the first floor in the Sala della Stufa, representing the *Four Ages of Man*, and five other rooms dedicated to the gods (Venus, Apollo, Mars, Jupiter and Saturn), allegorical symbols of the virtues pertinent to a prince.

In these rooms, next to the private apartments of the princes, the Palatine Gallery was set up, originally consisting of about five hundred paintings from the grand-dukes' private collection. The Pitti Palace has a Baroque interior (although some rooms are decorated in the Neo-Classical style, for example the Sala Bianca, and the rooms housing the Meridiana gallery) and contains the gallery with its remarkable collection of paintings including masterpieces by Raphael, Andrea del Sarto, Titian, Rubens and many others. The atmosphere of the court still lingers on here, indeed the palace constitutes the supreme monument of grand-ducal and royal Florence, the antithesis of the sober taste of republican, renaissance Florence. But it should be remembered that the grand-dukes preserved the austerity of Brunelleschi's style when they enlarged the palace facade, despite their taste for the contemporary Baroque style.

Behind that powerful stone facade, the many rich halls of the palace were witness to the melancholy and colourless lives of the last of the Medici. The interminable life of the bigoted Cosimo III (1642-1723), who received his guests in cold rooms ("he would never heat himself by the fire" says a contemporary source) and every day visited at least five or six churches; the brilliant life of his son Prince Ferdinand, impassioned patron of the arts, who eventually died of cerebral syphilis; and the dissolute life of his second son Gian Gastone (1671-1737) the last grand-duke. Gian Gastone was a pathetic figure, an open-minded reformer who, in reaction against the austerity of his father Cosimo III, led a debauched existence, hiring the infamous "ruspanti", young boon companions rewarded by a weekly "ruspo" (a Florentine coin). Lent was succeeded by a rather dubious carnival, and Gian Gastone ended his life, lying day and night in a filthy bed in the room that had been the scene of happenings worthy of today's pornographic trend. The last member of the family was the haughty Anna Maria Ludovica (died 1743); it was due to her that the Medici collection in which the specialists show such interest today, was not removed from Florence.

Of the Lorraine, who succeeded the Medici, the great Peter Leopold preferred to live in the Villa on the Poggio Imperiale, on the outskirts of the

Peter Leopold of Habsburg Lorraine with his family.

city, where he worked indefatigably at his social and political reforms. He had a charming little palace in Piazza San Marco built for his mistress Livia Raimondi. The Pitti Palace was always cared for by the Lorraine, especially by Ferdinand III and Leopold II, and the House of Savoy succeeded them as owners of the building. Victor Emanuel III of Savoy, King of Italy, donated the Palatine Gallery (which had been open to the public ever since 1828) to the Ministry of Education, and later in 1919, gave the whole palace to the state.

On the second floor of the palace, where Leopold II lived and where the famous Palatine Library was housed, the Gallery of Modern Art was set up, with the paintings moved from the Academy. The main part of this collection consists of paintings by the well-known *Macchiaioli*, a group of artists in Florence towards the second half of the nineteenth century, who "preceded in time, but not in temperament the Impressionists, with whom they have little in common" (Argan). In any case, for the Florentines, the Macchiaioli, with their lively and at times poetic realism, were the last original group of painters to emerge in Florence.

Henry Moore,
"King and Queen".

For the future, there is a plan to offer the visitor, tired after a tour of the vast museum complex of the Pitti Palace, after traipsing past kilometres of paintings and other works of art, a well-deserved resting place in a restaurant overlooking the Boboli Gardens, the splendid park which covers 45,000 square meters and which takes at least three hours to visit. There is also a project for a funicular which would carry the visitor from Boboli to the Belvedere Fortress which overlooks the city on one side and the hills of the countryside on the other. It is an extremely beautiful spot which would make a perfect conclusion to a first visit to Florence; its star-shaped design is contained within thirteenth-century walls, and the white building, by Buontalenti, still shows all the sobre and refined elegance of Florentine Renaissance architecture. On the other hand, one can feel how the fortress belongs to a coherent system which, as we have seen, includes the Pitti Palace, the Uffizi and the heart of the city, the Palazzo Vecchio. The fortress also occasionally houses exhibitions, such as the 1972 show of Henry Moore's sculpture. This show had a great success with the public, who particularly appreciated the open-air setting of some of the larger pieces; the local newspaper, however, was bombarded with letters of protest at this excessive evaluation of Henry Moore's "rocks" as these opponents of his art called them. It is not easy to overcome the diffidence and the sarcasm of the Florentines, but, one must admit, that their attitude can be partly justified by the fact that they are the heirs of the civilisation and the inhabitants of the city which can be seen from Belvedere.

Contents